LONER

LONER

INSIDE A LABOR TRAGEDY

BERNARD LAGAN

ALLEN&UNWIN

First published in 2005

Allen & Unwin
83 Alexander Street
Crows Nest NSW 2065 Australia
Phone: (61 2) 8425 0100
Fax: (61 2) 9906 2218
E-mail: info@allenandunwin.com
Web: www.allenandunwin.com

National Library of Australia
Cataloguing-in-Publication entry:

Lagan, Bernard, 1953– .
    Loner : inside a Labor tragedy.

    Includes index.
    ISBN 1 74114 515 5.

    1. Latham, Mark, 1961– . 2. Australian Labor Party –
    History. 3. Political parties – Australia – History. 4.
    Political leadership – Australia. I. Title.

324.29407

Set in 12/15 pt Bembo by Midland Typesetters, Maryborough, Victoria
Printed by Griffin Press, Adelaide

10 9 8 7 6 5 4 3 2 1

For Kay Lagan, my most beautiful mother

Contents

Prologue

On mid-winter's longest nights, dawn comes with a sapping chill over Launceston, Tasmania's northern city at the narrow head of the jagged Tamar Valley. The valley walls kill the wind and trap a low, thickening fog. The city's cafes steam over, breath puffs into little clouds and the sun struggles for strength on days shortened by the southern latitude. A European would feel at home in this enclosed, verdant, damp place. Like its weather, Tasmania is an island of masked influences; a gothic wet wilderness with a troubled past bred of its brutal treatment of convicts and, some say, the extermination of an Aboriginal population. But, of course, Launceston is also urban Australia and tuned to the same influences as any decent sized mainland town. In spring the north wind comes, warmed by the great Australian mainland deserts. It slipped in on 9 October. The temperature in Launceston hit 20.2°C. It was election day in 2004.

On that poll's eve Tim Gartrell, the federal Labor Party's mop-headed, boyish federal secretary, sat in his airy Canberra office beneath a wall of irreverent pictures of past Labor prime ministers—Paul Keating sipping furtively on a can of VB—and completed a last Friday evening task before leaving. He was close to exhaustion from directing the six week campaign, his first since taking charge of Labor headquarters a year earlier. There was nothing more he could now do for the party and its leader, Mark Latham. Gartrell had just seen the last of his party's private polling. It showed a surge in support for the Labor leader in the campaign's last hours; Latham's personal approval rating had lifted by three points and John Howard's had dropped by the same amount. Delighted by this late information, he quickly scribbled out his entry for the office's election sweepstake on a yellow post-it note and shoved it into a metal filing cabinet. Gartrell picked a net gain of seven seats for the Labor Party. None of the staff at Labor headquarters tipped anything less than a three seat gain.

The campaign's final day was a clingy, frantic Friday in Sydney. Latham and Howard darted across the city in a last round of radio interviews. Their paths crossed. In adjoining studios at radio station 2UE, sealed off inside little glass and gun-metal grey cocoons, they insulted each other on different programs to the world outside. Both wore their best dark suits that day and, when they came out, they smiled their camera smiles at each other. They had crossed paths at the ABC in Sydney earlier that day. Latham came in very close, peered down, grasped Howard's small, white hand and reeled him in like a fish so that the prime minister's head was at Latham's neck. He shook Howard's wrist with such force that the prime minister's body shuddered and he looked like a trapped creature whom Latham wanted to break. Latham's chief of staff, by now estranged from his boss, uttered, 'Oh, shit' when he watched the moment on that night's television news.

Howard scurried away to another station. Latham went to his old primary school at Ashcroft in south-western Sydney and stood in the faded cream classroom where he did the last of his primary schooling. He said he was proud of his Green Valley public housing roots and proud of the school that equipped him to have a shot at becoming prime minister. Then he went away and began calling nearly every small radio station in Australia to plead for votes. That night Latham took his staff to dinner at Aria, a restaurant overlooking Sydney Harbour at Circular Quay. He made a simple speech. He said the Labor Party had put up a good fight against John Howard's Coalition government but it would be hard for Labor to win. Still, most at the table expected Labor to gain more seats when the election was over. They were all told that the final Newspoll had Labor and the Coalition neck and neck.

In the late afternoon of the next day—election day—Tim Gartrell went back to the inner Canberra suburb of Barton to Labor headquarters. An election night war room was in one part of the building; in another, tables were laden with food and drink for a party. Gartrell went to his office with a couple of number crunchers and awaited the first results from a special computer linked to the Australian Electoral Commission.

At about the same time, Mark Latham, his wife Janine and his mother Lorraine drove through the thickening early evening light to the Mount Pritchard Community Club in Sydney's western suburbs fibro belt. The Mounties—as locals know it— is a totem to idleness. Canyons of gambling and video gaming machines beep, flash and spin inside an enormous, darkened mock cave. There are no windows. The world is outside. The Lathams went upstairs where the Labor leader's staff had been given offices for the evening. Latham settled down in the chief executive's expansive, grey den hung with framed posters of the hot-tempered British motor racing ace Nigel Mansell, whose driving career was marked by cruelly missed wins and spectacular accidents. The NSW senator John Faulkner and an election numbers man he'd brought down from Queensland for the night would be at Latham's side. Food and drinks were stashed in a nearby office. Downstairs expectant rank and file Labor Party members began lining up to enter another large room set aside for celebrations. A clutch of journalists had gathered upstairs around four television sets. Their conversation buzzed with the prospect of a Labor upset—or a calamity.

It was 5 pm in Sydney and Canberra but in Tasmania—the first state to move to daylight saving time—it was 6 pm and polling booths had closed. Counting would begin immediately and the results from the smallest booths would be known first. The Tasmanian timber towns fell fast—hamlets such as Smithton in the island's far north-west, a Labor town whose lifeline was the gnarled logging trucks that snorted past on the lonely Bass Highway. It swung by 14 per cent to the Liberals—proof, were it ever needed, that Latham's campaign pledge to seek an end to the logging of old growth Tasmanian forests would be a disaster for those whose livelihoods depended on timber.

The counting crept to the booths in the outer suburbs of Launceston—away from the direct impact of the anti-logging policy. It was with these results that those who knew where to look began to peer for a trend. Tim Gartrell saw it flash up on his computer in Canberra. Launceston's low-slung, brick and tile southern suburbs in the Labor held seat of Bass were on the move. Against Labor. These were mortgage belt suburbs, the places families sought out for their start. The largest booth in south Launceston, St Marks Church Hall in the suburb of Sandhill, fell to the Liberals. The young Labor MP Michelle O'Byrne had won it last time. Stephen Smith, a Labor shadow minister, was on ABC-TV's live election panel and he called Gartrell from the national tally room, also in Canberra, to validate his own dread. It was Smith whose doleful words then foretold the importance of what had happened in that church hall. He told viewers: 'The point was that most of these early booths were from out-lying areas, where you would expect the forest issue to run against us. The worst news I have had is that a big booth in Launceston itself has gone against us.'

The seat of Bass went to the Liberals first. Michelle O'Byrne tried hard not to cry. But she did. Then the adjoining seat of Braddon also fell to the Liberals. Labor's hard realists, such as John Faulkner, concluded very early that evening that Labor could not win the election with two seats gone in Tasmania. To win would require wresting fourteen seats from the government on the mainland. It could not happen. 'It's grim with a capital G and trouble with a capital T,' Stephen Smith told ABC viewers. Smith had seen enough in south Launceston to realise that the voters Latham had to capture in the outer suburban seats of Melbourne, Sydney and Brisbane would not materialise. Worse, Labor would lose seats in the big cities that night. Under Latham, Labor was going backwards. And John Howard would end up plugging more gaps in the ring fence of seats his Liberal Party had built through the outer suburbs of the big eastern seaboard cities since 1996.

Although Latham had acknowledged to himself on a sour, fitful night in a Cairns hotel room a month before that he would not win this election, the worst was happening and his mother cried for him. His wife was now very close to tears as well. Latham was indeed stunned at the loss of seats and remarked dryly to a couple of staff: 'Well, it's not going to be a night of shooting stars.' In the nearby function room, hundreds of Labor Party supporters watched a big television screen in sullen silence. They drank in sips, not gulps. Gough Whitlam came out to the Mounties that night to be with Latham. The former prime minister's eyes glistened over as he watched his protégé, who had enlivened politics since becoming Labor leader ten months before, limp through his concession speech like a grey and stricken man, his self leaching away. Far from pegging back John Howard's dominance, Labor lost three more seats. And Howard would win control of the Senate. When pictures came up on the large television screen of Howard's supporters at the Wentworth Hotel in inner Sydney braying and drinking champagne, the Labor faithful began to drift off quietly to their homes.

That night Mark Latham left his young boys at his sister's home and returned with Janine and his mother to his own house. He stayed up into the early hours of the morning with his wife examining how it had come to this and what of his future.

And his colleagues had their own questions. Did too many women and some men see menace? A man with a shaded past, though it would be little different from the lives of most of his era? An obviously highly intelligent man with a distant, hard side that his first wife thought not right and that she must change? A young man damaged by the truth about the father he adored? Was that the seed of his troubling reluctance to take the advice of others, the making of the loner? Was not his ending of his ambition with a miserable press conference in a scrubby park the full disclosure of the graceless man who could never have been the includer and inspirer his party and his country needed?

Yet Latham had given the Labor Party courage where there had been a tired timidity. His new ideas replaced wearied, recycled, remixed themes. He struck out and set agendas where there had been none. He found new ground for his party to take and hold. He excited the Parliament and the people. He found a political language that could be heard. Above all, he gave himself. And for a time in 2004 the Labor Party went to heights it had no right reaching so quickly. Then it fell so far, so hard. So did Mark Latham.

Chapter 1

History's Burden

MARK LATHAM'S SPEECH WRITER, DENNIS GLOVER, WAS ONE of the staff in an outer office at the Mounties on election night excluded from his leader's tight little circle. Glover, a reserved historian in his early 30s and closer to the Left than the Right, had maintained a stoic, loyal silence during the year as Latham rewrote his speeches, sometimes scribbling 'crap' on his drafts. It was undeserved. Glover spent the early evening calling out to his increasingly despondent colleagues the first booth results from the Australian Electoral Commission's website for the marginal seats Labor hoped to pick up. But as the evening wore on his mind drifted to his boyhood, to Holt, the seat in which he grew up on the edge of Melbourne's south-east suburban sprawl. It reeks of the Labor Party like Holt's rust-stained, closed down factories. Here live Australia's highest proportion of couples with dependent children, the highest proportion of people employed in factories, the lowest in tourism. In the Keating recession years, Glover saw his father made redundant by the squeezing of the car makers in Holt and his mother pushed out the factory door when the local cannery shut. Now, it was leaching Labor supporters.

Glover thought Holt would be lost to Labor. In the end, it wasn't but the swing to the Coalition was 6.4 per cent, making it just another Labor held marginal.

But also within Holt's boundaries is Westfield's flashy Fountain Gate Shopping Centre which features heavily in *Kath and Kim*, the ABC's parody of middle Australia. Glover wondered how it had come to this.

In the weeks after defeat, he left Latham's staff and set out to find his answer. He reflected how at one end of the electorate—the Fountain Gate end—mums and dads would these days drop off their children at low fee private schools in imported Korean-made people movers. But at the opposite end—where he grew up—there was an altogether different Australia; one of stagnating house prices, high unemployment and waves of kids who dropped out of school into joblessness. This end, once the working class and now the working poor, stayed solidly Labor. It was those aspirational voters at the electorate's other end who were being lost to Labor—those people who now made Holt the most interest rate sensitive seat in the nation because more than half of them were paying off their homes. And without reassurance about the party's economic competence, they would be forever lost to Labor.

Mark Latham was one of the first Labor politicians to analyse the reasons for the loss of the party's outer suburban vote and to foresee the troubled future it would bring. He'd lived it. The Green Valley street where he grew up in western Sydney is one of those left-behind pockets of decayed public housing, broken down cars and wild kids. It is now a place where people on life's margins live. Its promise of a start where young families could go into public housing and eventually buy their own homes evaporated long ago. The occupants of the old Latham house are among the legions of the left behind in the outermost suburbs of Australia's large cities. Margaret Allen raised three children in the house as a single mother after the Lathams moved out. She is married to Barry, who is 58 and jobless. Margaret does unpaid work in a charity shop. It's unlikely they'll ever leave public housing. The only joy for a Labor politician here is that this area is still solidly Labor. But great swathes of other people have risen up and gone to the Coalition, leaving the Labor Party to those who stay.

Labor's loss of its outer suburban territory has been happening since John Howard first won office in 1996. Howard gutted Labor in the lower- and middle-class mortgage belt seats on greater Sydney's fringes. He ignited a flame on the city's far southern bush and beach boundaries that roared west through the hectares of new suburbia in the city's far southwest and then pitched northwards to Penrith and the Lower Blue Mountains where the upstart Jackie Kelly snuffed out Labor's twelve year grip on the seat of Lindsay. West of Kelly's victory, the whole of the Blue Mountains—old towns such as Katoomba and Blackheath that had been Labor strongholds—fell to the Liberals. The burning of the Labor Party finally ended in the north, up on the Central Coast, where towns that retirees had colonised—along with young couples fleeing Sydney's housings costs—turned to Howard.

At first, this was seen largely by Labor as an aberration in Sydney, with the city's bigger mortgages and its greater loathing for Keating. But, in his subsequent election wins, Howard only tightened the Liberals' grip on the defecting Labor territories. Then, in 2004, he took Greenway in Sydney's west from Labor and filled another hole in the Liberal ring fence that he was building around Sydney. The city's remaining Labor members of federal parliament were being pushed into an ever receding clutch around the city's inner suburbs, while a noose of Liberal MPs encircled them. It was possible to imagine the Labor Party strangling to death.

Anyone who silently asked themselves the question on election night of how it had come to this might have cast a glance at Gough Whitlam, stooped, walking stick in his grip, his face ruddy, shambling out of the downcast throng after Latham's concession speech. It was in Whitlam's era that the seeds of Labor's current despair fell. Perhaps Whitlam thought back to his own long night of anguish, to 10 December 1977 when he failed for the third time to lead the Labor Party back into government, cut down again by Malcolm Fraser. At 11 pm on that night Whitlam knew his career in politics was over and he told the nation before he went bed. Whitlam had delivered the party from another darkness but he slipped in the same place as Latham's first stumble on election night, the seat of Bass in northern Tasmania.

On 28 June 1975, voters went to a by-election in Bass to replace Whitlam's former deputy prime minister, Lance Barnard, who was cashing in his seat for a foreign posting. The timing was appalling. The Whitlam government was ragged and battered by the botched attempts to raise billions in petro-dollars, a wages breakout, a credit squeeze and increasing levels of unemployment. The people of Bass fled from Labor. Then, in November, Whitlam was sacked by the governor general Sir John Kerr, in the most dubious of circumstances. In the ensuing general election on 13 December 1975, the Australian people cut Labor down to just 36 seats in the 127 seat House of Representatives. All of Whitlam's electoral gains since 1969 disappeared on that tide. The conservative middle classes were by now scornful of Whitlam's ability to manage the economy, aghast at his government's naiveties and indulgences. In the generation they were raising, doubt about Labor would be planted.

Gough Whitlam led a Labor Party—and a government, in its earliest times at least—that lifted many spirits and perhaps even caused people to fall in love with it. It spoke with excited hope to ordinary Australians and the young whose dreams were being enlarged and emboldened by Whitlam's vision of a self-confident Australia taking a higher place in a world where boundaries were shrinking due, as much as anything, to the cut-price seats on the new Boeing-747.

Australia changed in a blink and all of it was a revelation following the pallid McMahon years. Whitlam moved swiftly to offer the chance of a university education on the basis of merit rather than money, to recognise China and to ban racially selected sporting teams from coming to Australia. He supported equal pay for women, put contraceptives on the medical benefits list, banished the British honours system and tried to find a new national anthem. The promise of these policies delivered to him a generation of young, bright, optimistic Australians who might otherwise have been Liberal voters. All important was Whitlam's opposition to having Australian soldiers in the jungles and deltas of Vietnam, which made these young Australians the shock troops of his December 1972 election victory. Mark Latham, then a public housing boy in his first year at Hurlstone Agriculture High School, a selective state school, would be perplexed by the self-satisfied boos of the grazier parents of his school's boarders when Whitlam came to visit his school. Their vision could see no further, he thought, than their selfish opposition to Whitlam's removal of an outdated farm fertiliser subsidy. That day would long stay with the boy. He would come to love Whitlam's bold confidence—arrogance, even—and his mother would see in Whitlam a father figure for her son.

Then Whitlam's government fell apart. Blindsided by the first oil shock in 1973, brought about by an Arab embargo on oil production, Australia suddenly discovered it was part of the global economy in which someone else had the power. The era of unbroken post-war prosperity was over. Whitlam had a cabinet largely made of men who assumed that the years of post-war growth would just continue. For them, the Labor Party stood more for the redistribution of wealth, and less for its creation. They were not men who understood the emerging forces of international capital and markets, of globalisation.

Fear hugged the middle classes as Australia's economic performance faltered under a wages explosion, rising inflation, bigger deficits and, eventually, increasing unemployment. The government was overwhelmed. The people sensed it. After three brief years it was over. Just an interruption to the 23 years of conservative rule that had preceded it and that had now returned with that tall patrician, Malcolm Fraser.

Whitlam stayed on as leader but carried the shadow of defeat into the 1977 election and resigned afterwards. Bill Hayden, the flinty one-time Queensland cop who studied for an economics degree by night, took over and set about rebuilding Labor's economic credibility. He would battle with self-doubt and another Labor messiah.

Ever since Bob Hawke ascended the steps of the Old Parliament buildings in Canberra in 1980 as the new Labor member for the Victorian seat of Wills, the mantle of the Labor leadership hovered over him.

Hawke had gone to Oxford on a Rhodes Scholarship and returned as a larrikin who wore his channelled good looks and flirty charm lightly. He arrived in Parliament as the people's champion, a reputation won by his advocacy for workers as the head of the ACTU, and at a time of new-style presidential politics—when the party leader's personality would mostly outweigh policies as the bigger influence on voters. There had never been a bigger personality marked out for the Labor leadership than Hawke. His was unstoppable. Hayden was on borrowed time. And Hayden's demons of self-doubt were returning. When he beat off Hawke's first leadership challenge in the caucus room in July 1982 by five votes, he hesitated before getting up to make a victory speech, whispering to a colleague, 'Is it enough?'

Hayden would resign on 3 February 1983, overwhelmed by the Hawke forces and four hours before Malcolm Fraser announced a snap federal election in which he had hoped to be facing Bill Hayden. Fraser crumpled and cried that election night. Hawke had led Labor back. His would be a government that owed its success and longevity to the heeding of Whitlam's failure. This was to be a government run by new Labor men— Hawke, Paul Keating, John Dawkins, Ralph Willis, the hard-headed Peter Walsh, who resolved that never again would a federal Labor government stumble on the economy. They wanted Labor to become the party of economic management. They were mostly well-educated and well-travelled, and knew that Labor could no longer take economic growth for granted in the way the post-war men of the Whitlam government had done. They decided very early on that Australians would see economic growth as the test of their success—growth in jobs, living standards and company profits. They also realised that economic management was about wealth creation rather than its redistribution. For a Labor government, it was a great shift in thinking. And one that would help deliver Hawke four election wins—far more than almost anybody had thought possible.

If Hawke, for the most part, was the public face of this new Labor, Paul Keating, slim, dark, silently sliding through the corridors of Parliament in his delicate suits raking always for chance and opportunity, was the artisan of its economic management. He was the Treasurer and within his office were political aliens; dark-suited men who sat behind Reuters screens and watched the markets. Keating had come to this position with no more than his school leaving certificate and a preposterous ambition that carried him into Parliament at 25 years of age. He was a listener and a learner. And he heeded those in the Treasury, the Reserve Bank, academics and business people who quickly urged him to deregulate Australia's financial system, embrace the capital of foreigners and prepare for the coming era of globalisation. Keating's decision in late 1983 to float the Australian dollar—albeit amid a currency crisis and opposition from the head of the Treasury—was an exchange of vows with the world's new money men. It signalled his trust in the international financial markets because, with the float, Australia's financial destiny would be assigned offshore. And it cast aside years of Labor Party faith in a regulated, controlled, centralised financial system as protection from the very men Keating had now embraced.

Keating liked to paint canvasses that entranced the newly numerate economic journalists, Treasury's young turks and the money market men. He spoke of unclogging the nation's financial arteries by unshackling the financial sector from regulation and allowing foreign banks to set up shop. The latter decision contributed to the unsettling binge in the mid to late 1980s of enormous private and corporate borrowings. By late 1984, Keating had been named the world's greatest Treasurer by the magazine *Euromoney*. The term would later drip with sarcasm, when interest rates nudged 17 per cent, unemployment went past 10 per cent and Keating airily dismissed confirmation of an economic slowdown as the recession the nation had to have. He liked to say that he had de-spivved Australia with those mountainous interest rates but the real question was how many of those spivs did he create?

The government's popularity tumbled. Hawke, whom Keating believed to be shaken by the young Liberal leader John Hewson, refused to go quietly. Keating finally toppled him in an early evening caucus vote just before Christmas 1991, having plunged in the first knife a year before when he gave his famous off-the-record Placido Domingo speech to journalists in which he said Australia had never had the great leader it deserved. If Keating set out to deliver himself into that void, then he was compromised by those many insular years he'd spent as Treasurer, living in spacious and tranquil Canberra, dreaming his vast dreams and indulging his love of architecture, antiques and Mahler. Policy went askew. Keating the Treasurer couldn't let go of his numbers and forecasts to meet the pleas of his staff to lead. He got bogged down in a misguided private investment in a piggery. He turned back to his dreams as his political saviour: a republic, a new flag, and a fresh oath of allegiance from which the Queen was banished and God rendered an option.

Keating chose 13 March for the 1993 election. He went into it with close to a million Australians unemployed, the regions in recession, ravaged Melbourne on its knees and his government written off by most of the country's political journalists. He knew many Australians had their baseball bats ready for him, despite signs that his One Nation infrastructure projects were beginning to stimulate a recovery and that unemployment was levelling off. Inflation had also been hauled in. Surprisingly, he won. People decided it was worth keeping Keating in power to avoid Hewson's faith in market forces and his plans for public spending cuts. That did not mean they had forgotten the recession, Keating's distance from them, or his arrogance.

Bob Carr would later describe Keating's victory speech that night at Bankstown in Sydney's west as one of the great Labor speeches. Keating was generous to those who had not voted for him and spoke movingly about his need to reach out to and lift the unemployed. They were sincere words of warmth and hope. But there was one line that received most of the media's attention. It would reverberate and then haunt him. He said his victory was for the True Believers—those Labor supporters who had never doubted he'd win. It set Keating up to battle for years the perception that the night's election win was for Labor insiders and for nobody else. Later he rebuked a caucus member who said Labor had not so much won the election as Hewson had lost it. 'Pig's arse, pig's arse,' Keating told him. Those baseball bats used against Gough Whitlam were never really put away.

Keating began Labor's last years in office transformed and exuberant, like a man who'd survived the illness he feared would claim him. There was a lightness about him: he had repudiated Hewson's New Right market philosophy, he'd won government in his own right and the hardest, driest economic decisions were behind him. He could expect to begin seeing the rewards to Australia of the new economy he'd moulded, to see, as he'd once put it, the blooming of the land. The man who liked to talk of the Big Picture now had a new, enlarged canvass with which to work. He made his boldest strokes when he persuaded a doubting nation of the great good that would come from passing laws to enshrine the High Court's decision that Aboriginal people were the owners of their traditional lands and when he pledged to go to the people and allow them a vote on whether they wanted the republic that he wished for.

Then exhaustion overtook him. He had been ebbed out by the slog of the years as Treasurer and, as his former speech writer Don Watson said in his luminous book of the years inside Keating's office, Keating felt at just 46 years of age that the job had come to him too late. And just as Australians were exhausted with Labor, so too did Keating come to be exhausted with them. The people never understood his great excitement over engagement with Asia, much less his vaunted new security pact with Indonesia. Alan Ramsey, the *Sydney Morning Herald*'s diamond-hard Canberra columnist, wrecked his decades long friendship with Keating when he wrote before the 1996 election that the people had had enough of Keating's formidable mouth, and that he'd squandered the reprieve he'd been handed three years before. Labor's ratty 1996 election campaign and John Howard's crafty gamble that the people still had their baseball bats ready for Keating sealed the Labor defeat. Howard did nothing to deflect their anger— other than promise them some relaxed and comfortable years. Keating was overrun at the 2 March election.

Nine years on, and after nearly a decade of economic prosperity, Howard is still in office, something that was quite unimaginable to anybody in that departing Labor government of 1996. Almost equally unimaginable back then was the notion that outer-suburban Australia would so quickly become John Howard's people.

It is hard to recall any recent politician who has spent as much time thinking about and writing about suburban Australia, grappling with its changing make-up and trying to recast policies to meet the emerging changes than Mark Latham. It was a lesson he learned from Gough Whitlam, who decades before was the first political leader to see that the future lay in the outer suburbs. Whitlam went out and won those suburbs by offering a local fix—better roads, footpaths, sewerage systems and public transport. Latham believed his party had neglected the outer suburbs after Whitlam had gone. He once spoke about some of his old Green Valley schoolmates, such as Michael Shiner, who had taken the trouble while adults to better their qualifications, and who now felt the Labor Party had walked away from their lives.[1]

Mick Shiner came from a large working family that had been active in the Labor Party. His dad was a union organiser. Raised in a white fibro cottage on a public housing estate in a hard patch of western Sydney, Mick moved his young family into a smart $0.5 million home. He and his neighbours lived behind a perimeter wall. 'If I was back on the tools, the arse out of my pants, I would be a Labor voter for sure,' he said. 'But once you got somewhere, you feel disenfranchised.'[2]

The Labor Party may have been slow to meet the aspirations of western Sydney's emerging affluence, but the marketers weren't. The perfumed, muted ambience of the department store David Jones returned to the cavernous Macarthur Square shopping centre in Campbelltown after an absence of some four years. Why? Because more than 16 000 people in the area were carrying the upmarket store's credit card. Not far from David Jones Mercedes-Benz opened a showroom. Four new cars were sold on opening day. Business has been steady ever since.

None of this was news or a surprise to Latham. Still, Labor's loss of suburban Australia continued under his leadership, even though for a period at least it had looked as if he might stem it. How did the man who wanted to inspire the aspirations of so many fail? How did his year of talking to outer suburbia about balancing work and kids, family incomes and raising children fail him? Were these people not once Labor stock?

They are not the professional classes or even the technocrats who've surfed the new jobs and opportunities of the bullet fast communications revolution. They are instead plumbers, builders, metal trades workers, middle managers, the self-employed, franchise owners, contractors and the odd consultant. Many are doing comfortably well under John Howard's growing, confident economy. The outer suburbs needed a story from Mark Latham that connected his social aspirations for a Labor government with their continuing good economic fortune. Did they see Mark Latham lunge and embrace Gough Whitlam hard at Labor's policy launch? Did too many couples see a sullen Keating at that same launch, then simply look across the table, tremble at their borrowings and flee to John Howard?

It was the choice of tactics over policy that led to Latham's vacuum on the economy, his failure to tell the story upon which suburban dreams are these days founded. He had secretly decided early in his leadership that he would not move onto the ground that John Howard had occupied for himself and made his own fortress—Australia's remarkable economic record. The nation was about to enter its fifteenth year of consecutive economic growth. Its economic performance had been the strongest in the industrialised world, unemployment was at a 29 year low. That decision to hide on the economy may well have been Mark Latham's greatest mistake. And those around him quietly seethed at his refusal to take advice.

Chapter 2

One Bloody Wednesday

JUST AFTER 8 PM ON THE LAST WEDNESDAY IN NOVEMBER 2003, the Labor leader Simon Crean was at Tim's Chinese Restaurant in the Canberra suburb of Forrest with company he normally didn't keep. He was in the lair of his factional enemies—the Labor Left—celebrating the 49th birthday of the Sydney MP Daryl Melham when his mobile phone rang. A gravelly voice said: 'Johnny and I want to see you.' Crean thought his caller, the Victorian Labor frontbencher Martin Ferguson, wanted a meeting to discuss tactics for the last week of Parliament. When he realised Ferguson was calling from the Parliament House office of the Labor Senate leader and party powerbroker, John Faulkner, he became anxious, but told Ferguson to call back later.

An hour earlier Crean had been ruffled when a press gallery journalist, ABC-TV's Jim Middleton, led the evening news bulletin with an item that named senior Labor politicians who had been meeting to discuss Crean's floundering leadership. Middleton, who had been the ABC's chief political correspondent in Canberra for nearly fifteen years, reported that they had discussed who might be best placed to replace Crean if or when they told him he no longer had the backing of the majority of his parliamentary party. He told viewers that Labor's senior figures were weighing up whether to reinstall the former leader and two-time election loser, Kim Beazley, or to go for a younger man such as Western Australia's Stephen Smith or the Queenslanders Wayne Swan and Kevin Rudd.

Had it been about any other Labor leader, Middleton's report would have ignited frenetic activity within the 250 strong Canberra press gallery, especially among the morning newspaper journalists who had two or three hours to confirm the story before deadline. But Crean's leadership had been festering all year and most of the press gallery knew that Labor's heavyweights—Middleton had named Faulkner, the Victorian Senator Robert Ray and the ACT's Bob McMullen—were despairing over Crean's failure to lift his party. They also knew caucus was fractured in all directions over the leadership. Should Crean go? Who should replace him and when? To many, it seemed Middleton's story was just another phase of Labor's leadership agony.

The story did not go unnoticed in the offices of most Labor MPs and senators. Mark Latham, who had not been identified in Middleton's story as a leadership contender, dropped into Crean's office. Having long pledged loyalty to Crean, he left with the view that nothing was imminent. Crean's shadow Treasurer then went out and had a long-planned dinner with his staff on Canberra's bustling Manuka restaurant strip.

John Faulkner had also seen Middleton's story. So had Martin Ferguson. They spoke after Middleton's story went to air.

Faulkner, certainly, had not intended to see Simon Crean that night. He didn't know the source of Middleton's story, although he had his suspicions about a senior member of Crean's shadow cabinet. The story would now force a confrontation. Not only could Faulkner and Ferguson see the broadcast fanning the Labor leadership issue to the point where, again, Labor's messages would be drowned out for the year's last sitting of Parliament, but that day's issue of *The Bulletin* carried two long feature stories on the Labor leadership crisis. In one, Gough Whitlam said that Latham should succeed Crean—albeit after the next election. Another reported that the NSW premier, Bob Carr, was favouring the party's Foreign Affairs spokesman and urbane former diplomat, Kevin Rudd.

Ferguson called Crean at the restaurant again. He now made clear what he and Faulkner had discussed; for the first time in the history of the Labor Party they wanted to dump a leader before he had been allowed to contest a federal election. Ferguson suggested they meet in Crean's office in Parliament House. 'You have to be fucking joking,' Crean exploded at Ferguson. Didn't Ferguson know press gallery reporters probably had Crean's office staked out as a result of Middleton's story? They agreed to meet at 9.30 pm in the tree-shrouded, brown bungalow in the inner Canberra suburb of Narrabundah that Crean shared with fellow Labor men, South Australian senator Nick Bolkus and Northern Territory MP Warren Snowdon, both of whom were with him at the dinner. Crean told his companions about what was going on. They were shocked. Nick Bolkus, stunned, dropped a dim sim into the soy sauce bowl, splattering the others. The gathering moved into a sombre appraisal of Crean's chances of survival. It was a surreal scene: Crean was being knifed by his factional mates in the Right and being comforted by the Left.

Faulkner had come to the view in the previous few days that Crean's leadership was untenable. He knew, because he'd been sounding out Labor MPs, that Crean could not survive a caucus ballot. He also knew that sooner or later he would have to tell Crean that he had lost the support of the Labor caucus. He was increasingly fearful for the Labor Party that Crean's leadership would survive the coming Christmas break and carry over into Labor's national conference, due to be held amid the steel and glass of Sydney's Darling Harbour Convention Centre at the end of January. The convention centre was a bold choice for the ALP conference because it most often hosted glittering corporate functions, but would now be used to hone the vibrant, modern image Labor wanted to present to the Australian people at the start of the 2004 election year. Except that Crean had become the antithesis of that image. Focus group polling conducted for the Labor Party's head office was showing that voters were not just being turned off by Crean, they were getting angry with him. Faulkner and others worried that the national conference would degenerate into an ugly effort to mortally wound Crean and finish off his leadership. Such a public spectacle would be a disaster from which the party might take years to recover.

A senator for nearly fourteen years, Faulkner, from the ALP's Left, is a respected figure across the party's factions. The lanky, unrushed persona seen in public belies his toughness. Uncommonly for a politician, Faulkner loathes publicity. It has fallen upon him most often for the forensic manner in which he carves up public servants in Senate committee hearings. His co-assassin, Martin Ferguson, is also a gruff factional leader, one of three sons of the former NSW deputy premier Jack Ferguson. This is a political dynasty that makes and breaks Labor careers. Equipped with an economics degree, Martin rose rapidly through trade union ranks to become president of the ACTU—his predecessor was Crean—before entering Parliament in 1996. He was immediately marked as cabinet material, if not for leadership. By mid-year Ferguson had decided that Crean's leadership was either terminal or close to terminal.

When Crean's assassins set off from Parliament to his house in Faulkner's anonymous blue Toyota Camry, there was a third man whom Crean did not know was coming. It was the Victorian right-wing powerbroker, Senator Robert Ray, a close associate of Faulkner's and convenor of Crean's own power base in the Labor Party. The trio said little to each other on the ten minute drive through Canberra's empty streets. They reflected on what a miserable task lay ahead of them. Simon Crean is a thoroughly decent man whose life has been the Labor Party. He is no mere foot soldier. He'd qualified in the law and economics and brought a tough intellect to the party. His poor communication skills were, however, his downfall. If there was any doubt within Crean's mind about the extent of his loss of support among Labor MPs, then he was shaken when Ray's big frame walked through his front door. Crean silently reflected that Ray had once told him that he would be the first to know when he withdrew his support. It was not an undertaking Ray had kept. Crean was ambushed in his own living room.

In truth, however, Crean had been drowning for months. The *Sydney Morning Herald*'s acerbic political writer Alan Ramsey had a year before told his readers there was a hearse parked in Crean's driveway waiting to cart off the stricken leader's corpse. And there was no shortage of pall bearers. While he had renounced the Labor leadership to Crean after losing a second election to John Howard in 2001, Kim Beazley wanted it back again. He watched Crean's failure to ignite the public's interest. This was despite Crean turning his back upon Beazley's much criticised small policy target strategy. Crean had made a big, bold Budget reply speech in May in which he promised that a Labor government would lift Medicare rebates for all Australians and would aim for 80 per cent of doctor visits to be bulk billed. He promised to spend millions to save the once great inland waterway, the Murray River. But it was to no avail. In May, 60 per cent of voters declared themselves dissatisfied with Crean's performance as Opposition leader according to *The Australian*'s Newspoll. Leadership questions overshadowed almost everything Crean said and did. The same month internal polling conducted by the NSW Labor Party was leaked to the *Sydney Morning Herald*. It forecast a catastrophic result in five of Labor's NSW federal seats if the party went to an election under Crean.

If the leaking of the polling was intended to further destabilise Crean, then it worked. The Queensland front-bencher Wayne Swan said publicly that the party was headed for a train wreck under Crean. Beazley, openly endorsed for another tilt at the leadership by the former Labor prime minister Bob Hawke, launched his first challenge in mid June 2003. His supporters argued that John Howard's decision in early June to stay on indefinitely as leader of the Liberal Party— thus frustrating the bursting leadership ambitions of his deputy and Treasurer Peter Costello—meant that Beazley should be brought back. Only Beazley could take on Howard, his supporters argued. Crean's supporters countered that Beazley had already lost two elections against Howard. He'd likely lose a third. On Monday 16 June 2003, Labor's federal parliamentarians voted. Crean beat Beazley by 58 votes to 34 and Beazley said he would not challenge again.

That night as some ninety government and Opposition MPs dined at their respective ends of the parliamentary dining room, they watched ABC–TV's Fran Kelly report on that day's Labor ballot. She quoted an unnamed Beazley supporter: 'When it came to it, the turkeys voted for Christmas.' The government MPs roared with laughter. The Labor MPs sat sullen. The caucus ballot solved nothing. Crean failed to lift his own or his party's stocks. The public seemed largely disinterested. The Labor Party stumbled on through another dismal Canberra winter.

Elsewhere in Canberra, at the ALP's national headquarters in the leafy suburb of Barton, alarm set in over that winter. Labor's national secretary Geoff Walsh and his young deputy Tim Gartrell believed that Howard, having decided not to hand over to Costello, would now capitalise on Labor's awful year by going to an early election before Christmas. They quietly put their headquarter's staff on a war footing, ready for a snap campaign. But Howard, to their amazement, didn't act. They considered he'd made a big mistake. But just how wretched that winter was for Labor was brought home to Walsh and Gartrell one grey Canberra morning when they briefed Crean's shadow cabinet on the results of Labor's private polling. As usual, the results weren't good. The pair saw members of the shadow cabinet leave the room while they were still talking and they realised they were going outside to phone the results down to the press gallery. Walsh and Gartrell were appalled. They resolved to keep all future party polling away from the parliamentary party and, depressingly, they realised that the undermining of Crean signalled that another leadership crisis could not be far off.

In September, Gartrell, who was still in his early 30s, ascended to the top job at Labor's national headquarters. Born in country NSW, warm and mild-mannered, he was not in the mould of the blunter of his predecessors. His background was in the Left of the party. On a late November morning, Gartrell made his way up to Parliament House and to Crean's office. He had an unpleasant task and saw little joy in the day. The monthly private polling commissioned by head office now showed that the party was in a diabolical situation. John Faulkner and Crean's chief of staff, Mike Richards, came in as Gartrell began to tell Crean of Labor's peril. Faulkner was there because of his ability to keep his own counsel and his advice was well regarded by Crean. Nevertheless, Gartrell ensured that no papers showing the polling could be photo-copied and leaked. Instead, he beamed the disaster onto Crean's white office wall with a projector. Labor's electoral situation was virtually irrecoverable, Gartrell said. Labor would lose a staggering thirty or so seats if an election were to be held then. Crean was taking the party to an electoral holocaust.

Crean, slumped in his chair and stunned, did not contest what the polling said. He said he believed the continued undermining of his leadership by those MPs closely associated with Beazley was damaging him the most. But he said he realised his style and language were jarring with voters and he'd work to change that. They'd heard it all before. Crean had been told repeatedly by senior colleagues—such as Martin Ferguson—that his often carping performances before the media, particularly in parliamentary question time, were causing people to flee the party. Specifically, Crean had been told not to rise to the government's bait in Parliament because, when he did, he looked shrill and out of control. But Crean could not help himself. And now he was considered by some of those close to him to be angry and obsessed with those he believed to be undermining him—the likes of Wayne Swan, the Western Australian MP Stephen Smith, and the Victorian senator Stephen Conroy. Crean, some of his colleagues feared, was deluded, still believing he had enough caucus support to survive. And they feared he would take the Labor Party down with him rather than give his enemies the satisfaction of his resignation.

The minds of those who knew of the carnage that the internal polling said the Labor Party faced under Crean turned to survival. They decided to try and draft Labor's most successful and longest-serving premier, Bob Carr, into the leadership of the federal parliamentary party. It was done with great secrecy and those behind it believed that Carr came very close to going to Canberra.

There were no approaches to Carr—one at the level of the NSW party machine and another led by John Faulkner. It was clear to Carr that the overtures to him had been canvassed with factional leaders and had the support of the most of the Centre faction, the Left and some within the NSW Right. Labor's then NSW State secretary, Eric Roozendaal, led off the mission when he met with Carr in late September and urged him to resign as premier and move into federal politics. Carr recorded the approach in his diary:

Eric saw me yesterday to say do it. His plan would have me taking over the leadership, on the eve of the election, 'the first Opposition leader not even to sit in the House of Representatives'. He says he would raise a million dollars in the first week. His polling showed four in ten Liberal voters in Monaro say they would consider switching if I, not Crean, led the party. 'Run in Kingsford Smith,' he says. 'We'd take it off Laurie.'

Carr was also told by Roozendaal that Leo McLeay, the long-serving Sydney MP, might vacate his seat, and that he could probably expect about 80 per cent of the Labor caucus to support him into the leadership if he agreed to go to Canberra.

John Faulkner, unaware of Roozendaal's approach, also called Carr in late September asking for a meeting to talk about the parlous state of the party. They agreed to meet at Carr's Sydney home during the weekend of NSW Labor's October party conference. Carr's diaries record the meeting on Monday 6 October 2003:

> John Faulkner, Labor leader in the Senate arrives at 9.30 am yesterday to sit in our lounge room and offer me the leadership of the Federal Parliamentary Labor Party and a fighting chance of the Prime Ministership. He even offered his own job, that is becoming leader of the party in the Senate—a base from which I could run for a House seat as leader of the party, installed in the leadership on the eve of the election.
>
> He said Crean is fading fast, Beazley moving to succeed him, but that's just a return to the past with its own set of problems. Polling shows the election is winnable although Howard has a war chest surplus of $7 billion. Polling also shows a huge lead for Labor on health and education.
>
> John Faulkner says polling indicates the Opposition front bench is well regarded. Even Latham is seeing positive figures rise above the negatives. His key proposition is that the next generation, Swan, Smith, Latham, is not ready. He says there is a case for an outsider and I am it.

I run through the arguments against, it's too hard, I wouldn't want to let the party down, a transfer too awkward. He hints at the possibility of a party draft, even Crean asking me to take it on. He suggests my rejection is not entirely emphatic. 'I am being polite,' I say. 'Maybe part of me wants to entertain it.' He says: 'Who would it take, sitting here, to persuade you?' 'Maybe some definitive qualitative polling, not something rigged by the party . . . but even then . . . no.'

Friday Oct 31: Faulkner saw me again today with polling that he had the National Secretary commission. 'Only five people know about this,' he said. And he kept the copies, I didn't even make a note. There was a quantitative and qualitative report, Crean's disapproval is something like 62 per cent, he therefore has a massive net negative rating, Howard's net rating is only something like plus 10, mine is plus 40 (from memory—hard to recall). He says he tipped the last two elections with Kim. He thinks I can beat Howard (as the polling sort of indicates) but certainly rescue Federal Labor from a wipe out and win next time. Faulkner asks me whether I can be persuaded, who else can he get to talk to me? I say 'look, my self doubt hasn't shifted, I think the job is beyond me.'

I am impatient to go into the conference room and tape an interview for the Sunday program, so I agree to talk to him next week. If I continue to say no then he and Robert Ray will look at someone else (Beazley? Rudd?) but I intend to say no.

Carr did refuse to go to Canberra.

On that late November night as Faulkner, Ferguson and Ray confronted Crean in his Canberra home, it seemed the fears that Crean was deluded about his support were true. When the trio told Crean a majority of the Labor caucus wanted a leadership spill, this struck him as a clever choice of words. He said he believed he had the numbers to win a leadership ballot. He also said a majority were in favour of a spill because they wanted to settle the leadership issue in his favour. The trio replied that Crean should consider his position in the interests of the Labor Party. They said they believed he no longer had the numbers to win. Crean wanted to know from them who else had decided to withdraw their support.

'Obviously, you have,' he told his visitors.

The visit finished with Crean refusing to resign and with assurances from his callers that they would not speak publicly about the meeting. Later, Robert Ray would not be identified as one of those who had called on Crean that night—presumably to spare Crean the ignominy of it becoming widely known that his own Victorian faction was deserting him. After his visitors left, Crean phoned his wife Carole in Melbourne, telling her, 'It's on again. You'd better come up in the morning.'

Martin Ferguson found what he'd just done galling. His and Crean's paths had crossed in the highest rungs of national politics through the trade union movement. They had a shared history. Both were members of families who were Labor political dynasties. Ferguson went to the Canberra flat where he lives alone and rarely goes out when in Canberra. He called his wife, telling her, 'I've done it.' He would be despondent about politics for weeks afterwards. He fell out with his MP brother, Laurie, over the leadership issue and they stopped talking for awhile.

Back at Parliament House and in the restaurants and bars around Canberra there was great unrest following Jim Middleton's story. It was Wednesday night—the evening many parliamentarians go out and socialise before heading home from Canberra on Thursday. While only a handful of Labor politicians were privy to what had occurred that evening, most knew Crean's support was leaching away. They knew Martin Ferguson had decided to abandon Crean, as had Finance spokesman Bob McMullan, demoted as shadow Treasurer by Crean in favour of Latham. They had also seen Crean in caucus that morning make a desperate plea for an end to public bickering in the party. This had started after Latham went public with his support for tax cuts for higher income earners, remarks seized upon by the Treasurer Peter Costello, who had ridiculed Labor in Parliament by congratulating Latham on his stand. Crean's appeal to the caucus that morning had also been designed to head off an ambush of Latham by Beazley supporters, who sensed Latham might be a leadership contender if Crean was pushed out. To many, it was no longer a question of if, but how quickly Crean would go.

Before he went to bed that night Crean had a last, late night visitor to his house, the Sydney Labor MP Laurie Brereton. Long close to former Labor prime minister Paul Keating—with whom he shared a taste for fine clothes and elegant grooming—the former electrician, married to a Sydney barrister, quickly found a spot in Keating's cabinet. But, with Keating long gone and Labor in Opposition, Brereton's career had seen its best days. Always a classic backroom operator of the NSW Right, and well connected in business and politics in Sydney, his influence was now in career making. He'd survived for so long in public life probably because he didn't antagonise the enemies he made by talking publicly about his victories.

Around the time of the Sydney Olympic Games in 2000, Brereton decided Mark Latham, then a backbencher in exile, could no longer be left off Labor's frontbench. The party could not afford to waste his talent. Latham had fallen out badly with the Labor Party's then leader, Kim Beazley, over education policy during the 1998 election campaign and had taken himself off to the backbenches. Brereton went to see Beazley and asked if he'd bring Latham back to Labor's front line in Parliament—back into the shadow cabinet. Beazley replied, curtly: 'Next question.' But Brereton was determined. Beazley resigned the next year after losing a second time to John Howard and with the new leader Simon Crean installed Brereton renewed his push to restart Latham's career.

Crean, who wanted fresh blood on the frontbench, was cautious. He told Brereton he thought Latham should be brought back but that he (Crean) would not initiate a discussion with Latham. Latham soon approached Crean and Crean told him that while he didn't doubt his abilities, the issue was whether Latham could become part of a team. Could he drop his maverick tendencies? Latham promised Crean he would and Crean said he'd back him to return to the frontbench. 'That's good,' said Latham. 'Can you get me some votes?'

Within the Labor Party, it is the factions that decide who will be elevated, and Latham needed all the help he could muster. There were some objections even within his NSW Right faction. Two Sydney women MPs, Janice Crosio and Julia Irwin, were among those who told Crean they had reservations about Latham. They considered him too risky.

Brereton resigned as the party's Foreign Affairs spokesman and started working the numbers within the NSW Right to get backing for Latham to fill his slot on the frontbench. But the Right's old guard under the long serving Sydney MP, Leo McLeay, had its own candidates and Latham wasn't one of them. The showdown came on a Saturday afternoon at Sydney's Randwick Labor Club when the Right met to vote on who should go into Crean's shadow cabinet. Latham won the secret ballot, but there were actually two winners that day: the success in having his man elected ensured that Brereton was the new powerbroker in Labor's toughest, most successful faction.

Career making for his young protégé, Brereton set out on a mission to guide Latham into a position where he could one day make a bid to lead the Labor Party. He began speaking to MPs known to have misgivings about Latham, asking them to take a closer look. When Latham became Crean's shadow Treasurer in mid 2003, with Brereton's help, he also began appearing as guest speaker at many functions and fundraisers for Labor's backbenchers. Latham's capacities were being shown on a bigger stage and he was building support within the Labor caucus.

Brereton's grand plan for Latham, of course, was never announced and not immediately apparent. If it was not known to Crean, then Brereton did not enunciate it on the night he visited. Brereton—one of the very few MPs to become aware of Crean's earlier callers—wanted to know from Crean exactly what had been said to him. Crean set out for Brereton the plan he was hatching to stay as leader. He told Brereton he believed he could win a caucus ballot and that his assassins had been unmasked before they were ready because of Middleton's story. He believed they had not planned to confront him until the coming weekend—or possibly the following Monday, the eve of the last Labor caucus meeting for the year. Such a tactic would have given Crean no time to organise his supporters before the ballot. But now, Crean believed, he had been given a few precious days that those who wanted him out had not intended. He would use them well. He was thinking of ambushing his enemies by bringing on an early ballot, maybe on Friday. He told Brereton, 'Let's get the team together, let's meet first thing in the morning.' Brereton did not suggest Crean stand aside.

The next morning, Thursday, Laurie Brereton was on the phone—but not necessarily on Simon Crean's behalf. Mark Latham had come into Canberra early from the flat he owns in Queanbeyan—a town about 15 minutes drive from Parliament. He was taking a solitary walk around Canberra's Lake Burley Griffin when, at about 7 am, his mobile phone rang. He'd been expecting a call from his wife Janine in Sydney. It was Brereton. He told Latham of the events at Crean's house the night before, and then said: 'You have a very good chance of winning this.' Until then Latham believed that Crean, having reached the last fortnight's sittings of Parliament for the year, would survive as leader through Christmas and get a boost from January's national conference. The story of what had happened the previous night had not yet broken publicly. *The Australian*'s front page that morning was closest, reporting that Crean's support was bleeding away and speculating that there could be a vote on the leadership the following week. But the media had no word that the gun had been put to Crean's head.

Latham was interested. He knew Beazley, who had been keeping a low profile in Canberra but had recently embarked on an exercise regime in the gym of Canberra's Park Hyatt, would run against Crean. But Latham would not enter the race unless Crean resigned. He began to consider the prospect of Crean volunteering to go. He phoned Janine. She was keen. But when he spoke to his mother Lorraine, she expressed concerns, worried about the crushing demands of the Labor leadership on her son's young family. Latham asked her to see it as another opportunity, such as his getting through university.

Later that morning Latham met with Crean in the Labor leader's Parliament House office. The purpose of the meeting was to decide if Crean should fight and, if so, to draw up tactics. Crean's closest supporters were there. They included Western Australian senator Peter Cook and Victorian MP Julia Gillard. Brereton was also there. Crean maintained his defiance. He believed he could win, albeit with a margin as small as a couple of votes. His optimism was not shared by those around him. They reminded Crean of the standing within the party of those who had tapped him on the shoulder the night before. All were very senior figures. Was his position not untenable without their confidence? And what, the group asked, would be the scenario if Crean did just scrape back in as leader? He would be crippled and the party's agony would go on. The group broke up with an acknowledgment that Crean would reconsider his position during the day. It was a painful meeting for everyone.

In truth, those with Crean knew his cause to be hopeless. Most wanted him to have the time to reach the same conclusion himself. The killer blow came a short time later when Jenny Macklin, the deputy leader of the party, came to Crean's office and told him she could no longer support him. Crean felt like he'd been hit by a freight train. It was an emotional meeting. Macklin, who had been informed late the night before of the ultimatum that had been put to Crean, had barely slept as she tried to decide what to do. After her visit, Crean knew he had virtually no chance of fighting on. Some Crean loyalists were furious with Macklin, believing that the deputy was the leader's last line of defence.

The last supper came that night. Crean and his wife Carole went to Artespresso, a restaurant in Canberra's trendy Kingston, with his closest colleagues—though not necessarily any longer his leadership supporters. They included Peter Cook, Julia Gillard and Sydney MPs Daryl Melham and John Murphy. Latham was also there. The news that Crean had been told the night before that he no longer had caucus support was out. The press gallery was in a frenzy and, unsurprisingly in Canberra, the Crean dinner party was quickly hunted down by the media. Although Crean had virtually decided to resign—and Latham expected he would be running against Beazley— neither man had yet declared their intentions to the public. Crean invited a photographer from Sydney's *Daily Telegraph* inside to take a picture of the gathering, even hastily rearranging the seating so he could be snapped sitting next to his wife. 'It's always good to be with Carole and my mates,' Crean told the *Telegraph's* reporter.

In the absence of any public declaration, Latham's prominent presence in the *Telegraph's* photograph the next morning—Friday—was taken as another signal that Crean would resign and back Latham for the Labor Party leadership.

Ever since Crean had elevated him to shadow Treasurer, Latham privately believed he was Crean's choice as the party's alternative leader. After a short meeting in Crean's office that Friday morning with his close colleagues, it was finally agreed that Crean would announce his resignation at about noon, but Latham would not announce he was running until the next day, Saturday. The meeting was sombre. All were moved and impressed by Crean's stoic acceptance that he was being forced out before he could go to an election. They all shared Crean's determination not to hand the leadership on a platter to Beazley, whose supporters had run the long campaign to undermine Crean. Crean would work to shift his own supporters to Latham.

Before Crean's announcement, Latham got into his car and drove north on the Hume Highway toward his Campbelltown home in Sydney's south-west. From his car he called the former Labor prime minister Gough Whitlam—for whom he once worked and who had held Latham's seat of Werriwa for 25 years. Latham told Whitlam: 'Comrade, there will be a ballot for the federal leadership of the Labor Party on 2 December and I think the seat of Werriwa should be in it.' Whitlam replied: 'That's good, Comrade. Now I can die happy.' Later that day Latham also phoned another former prime minister. Paul Keating told Latham to get stuck in and take the party forward, not backwards.

Kim Beazley had, by chance, gained advance warning of Faulkner, Ferguson and Ray's Wednesday night visit to Crean's home. That morning, Beazley had wandered into John Faulkner's office to tell the NSW senator it was high time he and others with influence over Crean thought seriously about how long the Labor Party could continue to bleed under Crean's leadership. Beazley was attempting to persuade those to whom Crean might listen that the time had arrived to act. Faulkner was not specific, but told Beazley something was about to happen. Beazley, long experienced in Labor's methods, guessed the tap on the shoulder was imminent.

Beazley had decided early in the year that Crean would never lead the party to victory. When he learned of internal party polling in May that warned Labor would win just 35 seats in the 150-seat Parliament at the next election, he decided upon his failed June challenge against Crean. Now, at year's end, he believed that the best and cleanest way for Labor to resolve its leadership crisis was for Crean to stand aside and hand over to him. But he knew this would never happen and when Beazley confirmed that Crean had been asked to go, he was sure his adversary would put up fierce resistance and go all the way to another caucus ballot—one Beazley felt he might now win. But he'd not banked on Crean pulling out and delivering much of his support to Mark Latham.

Aside from the frantic activity in and around Crean's office on the morning after he'd been told he'd lost caucus support, Labor's Foreign Affairs spokesman, Queenslander Kevin Rudd, had a few discreet callers to his office in Parliament House. Among them were Labor frontbencher Bob McMullan and Tasmanian senator Nick Sherry. They were there to encourage Rudd to stand in the leadership ballot. Rudd, in his mid 40s, was a former diplomat and principal advisor to the one-time Queensland Labor premier Wayne Goss. Always carefully dressed—his blond hair giving him youthful looks—Rudd's command of his porfolio and urbane confidence belied his origins. His father, a share farmer, was killed in an accident when Rudd, the youngest of four children, was only eleven years old. The family were thrown off the farm and the young boy was shuffled between relatives until his mother found work nursing. Rudd's rise into Parliament from an impoverished background mirrored Latham's own story. His consensus style and considered manner were attractive to those in the Labor Party who didn't want to see Beazley resurrected, but were worried about Latham's unpredictability. Rudd believed he had the support of the three Labor premiers in the eastern seaboard states. Queensland's Peter Beattie had said as much publicly. Victoria's Steve Bracks and NSW's Bob Carr had given private indications to Rudd that they backed him to succeed Crean. Carr, who already had a strained relationship with Latham, kept his support for Rudd private as he did not want to offend Beazley.

Latham spent much of the weekend on the phone. He called about eighty Labor federal parliamentarians, starting with his known supporters, to let them know he would be in the race against Beazley who, by then, had announced his candidacy. Next Latham called the less certain members of caucus and, finally, those whom he knew would probably support Beazley or Rudd. He had two messages. The first was that the party needed to go forward, not backwards as would be the perception if Beazley returned. The party needed to make a generational break and elevate the post-Keating group of MPs to leadership positions. Second, Latham said that those Beazley supporters who'd undermined Crean—and the party—for so long should not be rewarded.

On Friday night, Latham told Janine that he believed the number of caucus members who had so far transferred support to him was in the low 40s. He needed 47 votes. He thought his support was 'respectable', no more than that. On Saturday he publicly entered the race when he called a press conference in the backyard of his Sydney home.

In Brisbane that Saturday evening, Kevin Rudd was also deeply preoccupied with the leadership contest. He had decided he needed to talk Beazley out of running. Using inter-mediaries he got a message to Beazley that he (Beazley) was in a hopeless situation and should drop out. Rudd's pitch was that if Beazley won against Latham, it would only be by a narrow margin. Beazley's authority as leader would be compromised and his narrow win would really be a loss for the party. But

Beazley refused to pull out. The next day—Sunday—Rudd decided not to put his name forward as a leadership candidate. He had two reasons: he now knew he'd come last in a field of three, which might compromise a future tilt at the leadership, and he feared he would be blamed if Beazley lost against Latham.

Late that Sunday morning Latham sent Janine, his mother and his young sons, Isaac and Oliver, on ahead of him to Canberra in preparation for Tuesday's ballot. Latham didn't want the family chased by the television crews he knew would be outside the house later in the day. They filmed him leaving alone for Canberra in the afternoon. By Sunday night, Latham felt he was marginally ahead of Beazley.

The next day, Monday 1 December, was surreal for the Labor Party. Crean, who was resigning, spent his last day as leader in the Parliament taking the party into question time. The government was in a generous mood toward Labor. John Howard announced money would be donated to a foundation for Alzheimer's sufferers founded by Hazel Hawke, who had been recently diagnosed with the disease. Crean's opening question on his last day as Labor leader was to ask whether the government would release children from migration detention centres. Howard played it with a straight bat and did not add to Crean's discomfort. Stoic in public, Crean was heartbroken over the end of his leadership.

The real drama of the day was taking place in the corridors and backrooms of Parliament as Latham and Beazley made their last pitches for votes. Inevitably, their paths crossed. When Latham walked into the office of Victorian MP Anna Burke, Beazley was already there. Latham quickly excused himself and left. The former Western Australian Labor premier Carmen Lawrence attended her mother's funeral in Perth on the eve of the ballot. She was grief stricken. It was a measure of just how tight Beazley's numbers were that she then flew the five hours to Canberra, voted for Beazley the next morning, and was on the way back to Perth when she learned the ballot result.

Laurie Brereton and Simon Crean were reporting back to Latham on his support in the NSW and Victorian Right. Julia Gillard and Laurie Ferguson were doing the Centre faction's numbers for him, while Senator Kim Carr was organising Latham's support in the Left. By the time he went to bed on Monday night, Latham believed he'd pulled ahead of Beazley by two or three votes.

Just before he left Parliament that night, Latham dropped into the office of Robert McClelland, a lawyer and the member for Barton. They were mates and often went out for a drink when in Canberra. Latham asked McClelland if he was going to vote for him. It was a painful question and McClelland had to tell Latham he was greatly worried about his maverick streak and he could not say he'd vote for him. Sensing McClelland's agony, Latham suggested he ring a mutual friend, Robert Stone, the CEO of Sydney's St George Rugby League Club and a former top player. Latham and McClelland were longtime St George supporters. Latham said no more and left.

McClelland came into Parliament very early the next morning—the day of the ballot—to play touch football. He walked off the field and called Stone at 7.30 am. Stone told him, 'If you go for Beazley, it would be like asking me to play first grade again.' Of Latham, Stone said: 'Sometimes mavericks can win the game for you.' McClelland took a shower and decided before he got out that he'd vote for Latham. Only later that day would McClelland realise just how crucial that decision was.

Latham had been waking earlier and earlier as ballot day neared. On the morning of the vote he woke up at 4.30 am in his Queanbeyan flat and went into the kitchen, careful not to wake up his wife, mother and children. He sat down at the table and began to write on a scrappy, single sheet of paper. It was the outline of the speech he would give to the Labor caucus if they elected him leader later than morning. On the other side he wrote the outline of a concession speech he would give if Beazley won.

Latham's sisters had talked about the ballot and didn't think their brother would win this time round. His second sister, Jodi, was at her Sydney home with her son Ben Mark Latham, aged eleven, and they sent a text message to Mark minutes before the ballot, saying not to worry. He would win next time. Shortly before 11 am Latham was elected the Labor Party's 18th leader by 47 votes to 45. If Robert McClelland had not voted for Latham, then the caucus would have been deadlocked. Never before had a shower scene been such an important part of a political drama.

Channel Nine's Laurie Oakes and Sky News—both with sources inside the caucus who phoned or sent text messages— went to air with the result before it was read aloud to the media gathered outside the Labor caucus room. The journalists present let out a collective gasp.

Latham made a generous victory speech and immediately moved to heal the party's wounds by inviting Beazley's backers into his new frontbench. He ate a simple takeaway Chinese meal with Janine in the Queanbeyan flat that night and fell, exhausted, into bed.

Chapter 3

The Sins of the Fathers

DON AND LORRAINE LATHAM RAISED THEIR KIDS IN A CREAM fibro cottage with a long, shady porch under a broad gum tree in Sydney's hard, far west. The little house still looks inviting, surrounded by Harrison Street's few scraggly trees, miserable Housing Commission flats and tight, little brick houses. The Green Valley public housing area was once a place of hope for struggling families, although Lorraine wept when Don moved the family there in the early 1960s. Mark was just four. They'd been forced out of their rented house in inner Sydney's Alexandria, close to where Lorraine grew up, because it had been sold. She did not want to leave. To her, Green Valley, 35 kilometres from the Sydney CBD, was as silent and lifeless as the Australian desert. The promise of new schools, community halls and playgrounds on the gum dotted, rolling farmland was no consolation for Lorraine, who needed gumboots to get through the winter mud to her clothesline. And the western Sydney summer turned Green Valley a withered brown.

Lorraine was a 19 year old working in an inner city box factory when she caught the eye of the foreman, Don Latham, in the late 1950s. He was fifteen years older than her and had already fathered two young girls in a previous marriage. Lorraine came from a strict, traditional family. Her parents were long-time Labor voters and her father, a truck driver, had warned her that if she ever voted for the Liberals, he would never speak to her again. Don, who never joined the Labor Party, had to fight hard for Lorraine. She was a reluctant bride and recalls: 'It took me four years to marry. I didn't want to get married.'

They did marry and three years later—in February 1961—their first child was born. They named him Mark. Three daughters, Tracy, Jodi and Toni, followed. By then Don was working as a technician at Sydney's Redfern Mail Exchange.

The family's little Green Valley house was dark. They cooked and ate in a tiny kitchen. The lounge was no larger than a decent-sized bedroom. Lorraine made a beautiful garden.

Her boy took to backyard cricket and his mother remembers the early signs that he hated losing. Once, when his grandmother bowled and took his wicket, he flung his bat and stormed off. Jody remembers that her older brother showed an early, fierce will to win the board games the family frequently played.

At his first school, Ashcroft Primary, Mark was usually first in class, and it was here that he developed a voracious appetite for books. He'd often come home at lunchtime, read, and trot back to school when he heard the bell ring. There'd hardly been a book in the house until Mark discovered the local public library. Jodi watched his progress through primary school and recalls: 'He was a really different child, really serious. To me he was quiet, intense, passionate when he thought about things. He had what I would call a bit of a presence about himself. We would have girlfriends over and they would say, "Who is that over there?" He would just say hello and be polite but he was always doing his own thing. He was very intelligent and today would be classed as really gifted.

He was just driven from within. There was no great talk about politics at home from my mother and my father. Just to work hard and get a good education.'

Don Latham developed big plans for his young son. He pushed him hard in sport and wanted good results at school. It was as if Don had seen a shining destiny in this boy when he was just a toddler. Later, Don's children came to believe that he might have been deeply frustrated with his own lot in life. Mark thought he would have made a good business executive. He was a clever man, capable of work beyond his technician's job at the mail exchange. As Mark grew older, Don would sometimes stay up very late playing chess with his son. It is easy to imagine that Don wanted Mark to be free of the limitations he experienced.

Despite appearances of a young family working hard to make its way, there was trouble. The children didn't know it then, but Don was gambling chunks of his pay on the horses. Jodi now thinks her father may have taken to gambling because of his frustrations. 'I think he was probably very intelligent. It was probably a thing of frustration not to have done better, perhaps. I think that's where gambling probably comes through, it's a way out, a quick way to improve yourself. But I don't remember him sitting there studying the form guide for days on end. I think it was probably big bets.'

Tension was developing between Don and Lorraine over money. There were muffled arguments some nights, often over the family's inability to raise the deposit for a home. Lorraine had taken a job as a school cleaner, leaving the house at 5.30 am to catch a bus to work and returning before lunch. Then she would be off again in the early afternoon for a second shift, getting home at about 6 pm. She would often tell her children, who put the kettle on for her when they saw her coming up the street, that the world was divided into workers and slackers. They knew where she wanted them, especially Mark. Lorraine thought early on that she had an exceptional son who could make something of himself. She told him this frequently, she nurtured him, she dedicated herself to him. Her expectations went far beyond those of most mothers in Green Valley.

Mark's sisters accepted their brother's special treatment. Jodi believes it natural that any parent of an exceptionally bright child would push harder. 'He was so intelligent—they really wanted this child to succeed,' she remembers. 'I suppose in any family if there is a swimming or running champion, the family all gets behind that person.'

In all families, there are different recollections and interpretations of events and relationships. The Latham family is no different. Jodi says her mother and Mark were the closest in the family. Lorraine has always acknowledged she leant heavily upon her son, but she has also rebuffed what she read as Mark's over-concern for her in later years. 'He said once, "you are my responsibility",' she recalled. 'I told him, "no I am not".'

The childen knew very little about Don's past or his family. It was not something that was spoken about. By contrast, in his early years Mark was very close to Lorraine's parents, who would drive out to Green Valley from Alexandria on the weekends. However, Don's constant doting on the infant Mark rankled with Lorraine's mother as she sometimes watched him ignore his daughters, walking past them to pick up Mark. Lorraine remembers a Saturday barbeque at the Ashcroft house when Don had some drinking mates over from the Green Valley Hotel. She told him that his frequent boasting of Mark's future might be wearing a little thin, but Don scooped up his boy and told his friends, 'He's gonna be prime minister one day, this boy.' Lorraine was right: some of Don's friends took to calling him 'Mr Mark'.

Indeed, it is possible that Don's expectations were a burden to his young son. After Latham was elected Labor Party leader, he invited Neville Smith, his old primary school teacher and cricket coach, to attend the 2004 Labor national conference, where Mark thanked him from the rostrum for being a mentor and for caring. Smith later suggested that Don might have overburdened his son, that he was a hard taskmaster and was often displeased with Mark's performance. Smith thought that the experience was both good and bad and had contributed much to Latham's makeup. This view is partly shared by Jodi. 'In some respects Dad, I suppose, was quite hard on Mark. It was in a male sense. Not in any physical way. It was school work and grades and it was my dad pushing him to do his best.'

Lorraine recalls Mark's later years at high school. 'He lived in his bedroom. I can remember his mates knocking on the window and Mark saying "no, I am not coming out". After he finished his exams, he said, "Mum, I don't want to leave school." He just loved learning.' Not once did his mother have to ask her son to do his homework and Lorraine cannot remember him ever taking a sick day while at school.

Unsurprisingly, Latham won a place at one of NSW's oldest state and best selective schools, Hurlstone Agricultural High at Glenfield. Built in 1926 on 330 acres of land, the school's centrepiece is a magnificent sandstone building with wide verandahs and a sharply gabled roof. Conceived as a school for sons of the state's well-to-do graziers, the farmers' sons who made up the ranks of the school's boarders were a sizeable presence when the boy from Green Valley joined them as a day boy. It was a big break for the public housing kid and he thrived in the classroom, finishing up Dux of the school in 1978. In his final year, he captained the school cricket team— scoring a century off 35 overs—ensuring his team won the Alan Davidson Shield (a competition in which about 400 NSW high schools competed). And he was also awarded a Hurlstone College Half Blue for his performance on the rugby field as a second rower.

The boy shone. It is possible to imagine that Mark was motivated by a terrible fear of failure. He had the weight of Don's expectations upon him, and he had his mother's frequent reminders that he would come to be judged either as a worker or a slacker. He came from a part of Sydney once described by Hugh Stretton, the Australian–born Oxford history professor, as 'among this century's most deliberate, unnecessary, concentrated and massive offences against Australia's children'. The need to find a way out was overwhelming. Education would be the means.

By his mid-teens Latham had earned a reputation not so in keeping with the quiet, studious boy he'd been at primary school. He'd developed a combative outspokenness at Hurlstone that irked some teachers. When he was a 15 year old in Fourth Form, Latham wrote a scathing article for the school magazine, *Harvester*, attacking the school's administration for waste and mismanagement, questioning where the pupil levy for school excursions was being invested. The language was intemperate. Latham's article ended with a provocative, even offensive jibe at his teachers: 'Maybe those ratbags [who] are a long way above our authority, most of whom probably don't remember what school was like, might wake up to themelves soon!!!'

Later that year, Latham wrote a more considered article, making the case for selective schools to widen the criteria for accepting students beyond just academic results. He wrote: 'From my experiences of these high natural ability students, only about 30 per cent of them are prepared to put the real effort into their education needed to produce the superior academic results that their natural abilities say they should be producing.' He said less gifted kids who showed ambition and effort should be included: 'In doing so we will be able to bring into selective high schools people who are prepared to work and achieve . . . such a modification relates to societies in general, for example Australian apathy (no effort) versus Japanese ambition and effort.'

Latham was 16 years old when he wrote those words. The passages echo with the boy's realisation that ambition and effort would carry him, and others like him, where he wanted to go, not privilege. This theme would come to define him. But, even back then, it may have been at a cost. Despite rising to be Hurlstone's star pupil and making the First XI and First XV, Mark Latham never became school captain. One theory is that while he had good support among the students, the weighting system gave considerable influence to the teachers, more than a few of whom voted against the young upstart.

It was before he went to Hurlstone that Latham first saw the man who would become almost as important in his life as his father. His name was Gough Whitlam.

Shortly before he entered his teens, Latham received an award fom Liverpool Council for outstanding school and sporting performances. Gough Whitlam, then leader of the federal Labor Party, presented him with a medal. But it wasn't until a few years later, when Latham was a 13-year-old First Form student at Hurlstone, that he took real notice of Whitlam—by then prime minister—during a school speech day. The unlikely subject of his interest was farm fertiliser. As Whitlam took to the stage the parents of Hurlstone's country borders—many from comfortable farming families—began to heckle the prime minister. They were annoyed that he had decided not to renew the government's annual $56 million superphosphate bounty which subsidised farm fertiliser. Acting on advice from the former Reserve Bank governor, Dr H. C. 'Nugget' Coombs, that farmers' incomes were at record levels and the bounty was no longer needed, Whitlam decided he had better ways to spend the money. Latham was transfixed by the spectacle, and vexed that some in the audience would treat the prime minister this way. The memory of that day stayed with him. It may well have stirred within him the first thoughts of a political life.

It was not until after he'd moved on to the University of Sydney to begin his economics degree that Latham came to realise the real extent of his family's circumstances. He began to feel what he has called a deep sense of urban injustice, brought on by the three hours he was spending each day commuting by train, bus and on foot between home and university. By then he'd also taken a part-time job at the Green Valley Hotel, picking up glasses and working in the bottle shop. When he began to mix at university with the children of the well-heeled from Sydney's eastern suburbs and the north shore, his sense of injustice became more acute. 'I remember talking to one of the north shore fellas at uni about what he was doing for his holidays and he was off to the snow for three weeks. I was off to pick up glasses at the Green Valley Hotel. Whether you call it anger or any other emotion, it certainly left me with that sinking feeling that society wasn't all that fairly structured,' he recalled.

Jodi Latham became aware as she was growing up that her family never went on holidays or rarely went to the movies. She says: 'In the area where we grew up, even though there were a lot of people doing it tough, we also had friends whose fathers worked and they went on holidays. So you knew as you were growing up there was something wrong. Our father was working but we weren't living the same lifestyle as everyone else. To me, I think he had an alcohol problem but he wasn't a raging drunk. There was no alcohol in the house. He probably just spent too much time in the Green Valley pub. Thinking back, I think he was more of a binge drinker—the people that start to drink and they just go for days on end, that sort of thing, where you would disappear. And, unfortunately on pay days, I would imagine that happened. But it wasn't all the time, it wasn't like we lived in this terrible home. He obviously had periods where he was okay and then he would sort of lose it again, I think. It sounds terrible, but he was still a fantastic father. Absolutely affectionate.'

While Mark was at uni, Don's health began to deteriorate and on a hot Friday in February 1981, he collapsed at work, hit by a stroke. Mark realised Don was going to die when his condition worsened over that weekend in hospital. He went to his father's bedside on the Monday morning to say goodbye. Don died just after Mark left.

When Mark returned home from the hospital, a letter was waiting for him from Sydney University. All his grief and pain were galvanised into the moment when he tore open the crisp envelope to learn he'd won the university's economics prize for second year students. Don would have been so proud. Mark was 19 years old.

Lorraine was devastated by Don's sudden death. Toni was barely 11 and Tracy and Jody were still at high school. She knew the family's financial situation was perilous. There would be a modest compensation payout as Don had taken ill at work. But their income would be meagre, gleaned from Lorraine's part-time work as a school cleaner and Mark's earnings from the hotel. The family owned virtually nothing, just their clothes and the household furniture.

It was then that Lorraine took her son aside to explain the reason for the family's circumstances. Don Latham had been a gambler, a punter. He'd lost a fair bit of the family's income over the years. To Mark, his mother's revelation was like the lifting of a veil. Much of what had occurred in the home—the tensions, the clipped parental murmurings—fell into place. It explained why Don's old used cars came and went, why there were no family holidays and why outings were seldom. It cleared up the mystery of where Don was at times and of what he was doing. It also caused Mark to make a painful reassessment of his father. Although he felt Don was a diminished man, his love for his father did not lessen.

The revelation about his father led Latham to a decision that would cause him good and ill in his years in politics: he resolved he would not make Don's mistakes. He vowed that in his own life he would quickly face up to problems, confront them and resolve them. Be strong. He would not let them fester and overwhelm him. But this decision, however noble, led at times to a dangerous impetuosity that would later skewer some of his political judgements, baffle colleagues and create enemies. It was Don's flawed gift.

Mark's first instinct after his father's death was to abandon his studies and find a full-time job to support the family. However, local Labor Party identities got wind of this and rallied around to find the money so he could stay at university. Latham finished university in 1982 with an honours degree in economics.

In early August 1987 Gabrielle Gwyther, a willowy girl from Bankstown, joined a dinner at a Chinese restaurant in Liverpool for the overseas bound brother of one of her girlfriends. Gwyther was 22, and a registered nurse who'd become disillusioned, angered and politicised by the repressive atmosphere and archaic work systems in NSW public hospitals. The pay was terrible and the work long and arduous. She had ended up organising the union at the hospital before she quit. She was now working in real estate.

The daughter of a pharmacist and educated with a feminist streak by the Dominican nuns, Gabrielle had long, wavy blonde hair and a broad, shy smile. She barely noticed the big man, a few years older than her, further down the table. But Mark Latham certainly had eyes for her. After the dinner, the party went to a nightclub behind the restaurant and Latham made his move. It was unusual. He dropped to the floor in front of Gabrielle and launched into a fierce round of push-ups. She was unimpressed and embarrassed and soon left. He was not the kind of man her family would have intended she go out with. But she relented a week later when Latham rang her up and asked her out.

Gabrielle decided early on that her first judgement of Latham had been too hasty. Here was a man, she realised, who really did want to change the world. She was captivated. But she also realised he had a hard side. Odd, even. Something was not quite right. She decided she wanted to soften him. It was something she could do for him. She was in love.

Later that same year Mark was elected to Liverpool City Council on the Labor ticket. He was 26 years old. The new mayor was Green Valley Labor identity Casey Conway, a stocky, warm, former boxer and plasterer. Conway, who was also one of the donors to the fund that kept Latham at university, vividly remembers the first caucus meeting of Liverpool's councillors after the election. The note he made in his diary read: 'At caucus Mark Latham was bombastic and abusive. He rejects opinion of the majority of caucus. Referred to me as a socialist and Paul Lynch was a supercilious cunt. How are we going to work in unity with this character?'

The Mark Latham Conway saw in caucus was very different to the student he'd helped through university, something Conway put down to Latham's involvement with Whitlam. Latham had taken on an arrogance. It only got worse and the local papers were soon carrying stories of fiery exchanges between Mayor Conway and the young Latham. Typical was a report in which Conway said of Latham: 'I have a son his age and if he behaved like him [*Latham*] to his elders, I'd give him a smack in the mouth.' Conway went on to complain in the newspaper that Latham was too blunt to Council staff and had a habit of foreshadowing reforms to the Council in public before discussing them internally. It signalled Latham's Gough-like faith that he could dictate policies with minimal consultation and carry the people with him.

Latham was certainly under Whitlam's influence by then. In late August 1982 he had interviewed Gough for his university thesis and Whitlam offered him a job as his research assistant. The former prime minister was in the throes of writing his

800-page memoir, *The Whitlam Government*, and needed help. The job would turn out to be even more exotic than Latham could have imagined. The following year Whitlam was appointed Australia's Ambassador to UNESCO and Latham travelled to Paris to stay with the Whitlams in their spacious apartment atop the Australian Embassy on the Rue Jean Rey. It was the beginning of a long and close relationship, one in which, according to Lorraine, Gough would come to be a father figure to her son. Gough nurtured Mark's career in the Labor Party. He taught Latham about the language of politics, about history and culture. He encouraged him into public life.

Out of this abiding relationship grew Latham's great convictions about how a political career should be conducted. In 1985 he set down in the *Liverpool Champion* what he had learned from Whitlam:

> Whitlam had one priceless quality in politics—to put new ideas on the deck, something the present bloke doesn't have. I've learned from Whitlam that unless you are prepared to take the initiative and lead the debate and sell your ideas to the public, the chances of getting through reform are next to nothing. You can't say Bill Hayden ever campaigned hard on an issue, or that Hawke has got ideas that he constantly tries to sell to people. They just seem to float along.

What is striking about those words is that within them rests the credo that marked his leadership of the ALP. And the very things that seeded his doubters and fuelled his detractors: his courage to be innovative, the preposterous self-belief, the desire to tear down and rebuild, the cool arrogance, the troubling impetuosity. All were part of the wings on which he was lifted into politics; all helped to bring him down. And all were played out in the early years following Latham's entry into Parliament, after Kim Beazley had made him education spokesman.

On a grey, wet early October morning in 1998, Kim Beazley was at the busy Frankston TAFE in Melbourne's south to launch Labor's education policy to an unenthusiastic gathering of staff in a chilly, austere library. It was about halfway through a federal election campaign that John Howard already looked like winning. The leaden skies suited the mood inside the Labor camp. As soon as Beazley had finished, a glowering Mark Latham disappeared out the door. He was in no mood to talk. He saved that until Howard defeated Beazley.

A week after election day, Latham went on ABC radio in Sydney and poured out what really happened on that miserable day in Frankston. His education policy had been butchered inside Beazley's office, he said. The detailed policy he had spent eighteen months putting together had been reduced to what he called a series of dot points, trivialised, gutted. And he had not been told why. He was quitting the frontbench.

He had rowed furiously with Beazley's office on the morning of the education policy launch. Big slabs of policy had been dropped including reform of middle schooling, plans for a more progressive university student contributions scheme and childhood development initiatives. Latham had not even seen the final education policy until he read a copy in the cab on his way back to the airport after Beazley had finished speaking. He resolved to say nothing until the campaign was over. Privately, Beazley's staff countered, Latham's policy document was unusable in the form he'd supplied it.

Explaining his decision to sit on the backbenches, Latham told the *Sydney Morning Herald*'s Alan Ramsey: 'The outer circle of the frontbench is no man's land. Well, I am out of there now. And some of them are wondering, what's he up to? Well, it's pretty obvious what I'm up to. I just want to get satisfaction back into my work.' Latham became a free public thinker, unshackled from the burdens of frontbench solidarity. He wrote columns for Sydney's *Daily Telegraph* and the

Australian Financial Review, and penned many speeches. They were often provocative, urging, among other things, a return to corporal punishment and sending troublesome boys to work farms. Or they were seemingly at odds with long-held Labor traditions, such as his advocacy of a crackdown on invalid pension entitlements and his support for moves to push teenage mothers into the workforce. Latham liked to tell the poor what was best for them.

One article he wrote for the *Australian Economic Review* in late 1998 stood out. Latham claimed the federal Labor Party was in a policy mess and that the inner circle of Beazley's shadow ministry equated economic efficiency with electoral death. The party was in an intellectual vacuum, Latham said. He included an attack on the NSW Labor premier, Bob Carr, when he urged federal Labor 'to avoid repeating the mistakes of Bob Carr in NSW; opportunistic in Opposition, followed by broken promises and pedestrian policies in Government'. Beazley's Labor Party, Latham wrote, was ruining the record of the Hawke and Keating governments because Beazley was offering corporate Australia a break from competition. Labor colleagues mostly suffered in silence.

Latham developed a reputation for poorly thought-out policy positions that were designed only to get him noticed. But he had, before the 1998 election, written an academically well received, if somewhat high-brow, book. He called it *Civilising Global Capital: New thinking for Australian Labor*. It underpinned his credentials for putting forward fresh policy ideas in a serious fashion. It showed effort, originality and guile. It established him in the public mind as one to watch. A bit of a maverick, but a very bright one. Kim Beazley launched the book although he was careful not to endorse its contents—which was really Latham's attempt to flag the agenda for a reinvented Labor Party. Beazley must have been uncomfortable with some of Latham's ideas, which included the proposal that more people should repay government handouts if and when they could afford to, that a bigger tax base was needed and that governments were too often blamed for the failings of incompetents in corporate Australia. Perhaps the book's most radical idea was that a Labor government should consider a progressive expenditure tax. Such a tax uses 'taxable consumption'—income minus savings—as the tax base. Within the vacuum of the emerging small target policy strategy that Beazley would use in his second attempt against John Howard in 2001, Latham's book seemed only to mock Labor's policy silence.

Beazley lost in that second attempt to bring down Howard. He had refused all overtures from others within his party to bring Latham back into shadow cabinet before the election because he believed that Latham 'had too much shit on his liver' to be resurrected and would be best left on the backbenches for a period, although he had planned to put Latham back in his ministry if he defeated Howard in 2001. However, Beazley's regard for Latham was to again diminish. Had he won the December 2003 leadership ballot against Latham, he would have replaced Latham as shadow Treasurer, the post Simon Crean had given him. Beazley believed Howard's Treasurer, Peter Costello, would have destroyed Latham. His first choice for the job would have been the Western Australian MP and Beazley loyalist, Stephen Smith.

Beazley's mercurial relationship with Latham was shared by many of his colleagues in Parliament. It reflected Latham's great abilities and his troubling flaws.

Chapter 4

Sweet Summer

FEBRUARY'S FIRST TUESDAY IN 2004 DAWNED COBALT THEN vivid blue. Little clouds lolled out to sea and a gentle wind ruffled the water's surface, tempering the early sun on the coast north of Sydney. Lone swimmers ambled down to the shore. It was a morning to warm any soul. Even the piffle on the sides of two buses in the nearby carpark of the Galaxy Motel at Gosford looked less a lie: 'Mark Latham and Labor—Opportunities for All.'

On the larger bus some of the bigger names of the Canberra press gallery, such as the ABC's Jim Middleton, the *Daily Telegraph*'s Malcolm Farr and *The Australian*'s Steve Lewis, settled into their seats. The Labor Party was recovering in the polls and these journalists had decided there might be some political history to be made in an Australia still lost in late summer. For the country's political journalists, it was the start of another of the years they lived for: election year. And this would be a contest between a young, inexperienced Labor leader and the old fox John Howard, who had decided to block the leadership claims of his ambitious Treasurer Peter Costello, and dash for a fourth term in The Lodge. Latham's elevation to the Labor leadership had been like throwing a jerry can of petrol on the contest between Howard and the Labor Party, which had remained moribund under Crean. Suddenly national politics was enlivened. This was a contest between the comfortably familiar Howard and a discomforting unknown. Between Howard's cosy conservatism and a club buster.

Mark Latham was aboard the smaller bus with some of his staff and the NSW senator, John Faulkner. On the media bus was Latham's new press secretary Glenn Byres, a laconic, lanky 30 year old who had taken leave from the Sydney-based political and lobbying outfit Hawker Briton, founded by former staff of the NSW premier Bob Carr. Byres was the linkman between the press and the Latham entourage, fielding requests for interviews and keeping journalists informed of the day's planned events. Once a press secretary to Carr, Byres managed to disguise the edginess he felt inside. Latham was on a high risk mission.

The buses were heading to the Gosford Leagues Club— the venue for the first of a series of old-style town hall politi- cal rallies where Latham would speak and then take questions. The buses would roll north all week—right to the Queensland border—stopping along the way for more public meetings. Latham talked up the dangers by calling it politics in the raw. The meetings were open to all comers. The Labor Party had advertised on local radio but no one knew who would turn up or what their mood would be. Latham had no written script and no handy briefing notes to fall back on for tricky ques- tions. He could not be seen to be avoiding questions in front of large, live audiences. Nor could he risk locking into policies and positions not yet agreed upon by his parliamentary col- leagues. The media would be there as would the Liberals, their observers in attendance to dissect the meetings.

The potential for the new Labor leader to trip up or, worse, lose control of a meeting could only help the Howard govern- ment in its efforts to portray Latham as an undisciplined, unpolished, wildly unpredictable upstart who would have a fleeting life as Labor leader. There was also the distant spectre of the comet-like former Liberal leader, John Hewson. He had used big, free-wheeling open meetings in the 1993 election campaign to pull in voters. It had backfired. His verbal brawling generated much negative television depicting conflict and anger.

Yet the public meetings were, for Latham, risks that had to be taken. First, there might be—depending when Howard called an election—very little time to get the new Labor leader out there and known to the public. He was not a familiar figure. Second, the Labor Party could not ignore the success that standing in front of the voters had brought to the Queensland premier, Peter Beattie, who would win another election in the week of Latham's first bus trip.

Latham really owed the idea to Con Sciacca, an adversary in the Labor Party. Sciacca, a long-serving Queensland MP, was a Beazley supporter who'd snarled at reporters as he emerged from the December leadership ballot. Afterwards, Latham went to him and held out the olive branch. He offered to come and campaign in Sciacca's marginal Brisbane seat of Bowman. Sciacca jumped at the opportunity and organised a community meeting later in December. Surprisingly, more than 600 people turned up. It firmed the idea in Latham's mind that this was a way to counter the feeling many people had that politicians lived lives remote from their own.

Political leaders often try to create the impression for television that what they are doing is somehow spontaneous and genuine when mostly they are operating from a tightly contrived script. There was, of course, a script to what Latham was doing. It had most recently been updated by the former US president, Bill Clinton, who in his first campaign against George Bush Snr had termed mingling with voters, town meetings. It was a script that was not predictable. Things could go awry, but Latham knew it was different enough to attract national attention. And it was something Howard could not do. He'd been prime minister for so long that he would be forced into a series of running defences of his government's many unpopular decisions. Latham's meetings were designed to highlight his accessibility over Howard's inaccessibility. New ideas. Youth versus age.

Howard's itinerary only helped Latham. That morning, the prime minister was on the other side of the continent fortified against accidents. He'd gone to Western Australia on a four-day tour of marginal seats. His rally in Perth was open to invited Liberal supporters only. Protesters were cordoned off and limited to shouting from a distance while Howard hurried uncomfortably past. He allowed himself a quick smile when someone shouted, 'Not fucking happy, John!' This was merely more of the tight control minders on both sides of politics have used increasingly over the last decade to shield political leaders from unwelcome incidents that might throw them 'off message'.

The control had been temporarily suspended for Labor. A woman called Keri-lea Menzies screeched in the change on day two of Latham's tour. She grabbed the microphone at his second community meeting—in Raymond Terrace outside Newcastle—and harangued the Labor leader over his plans to encourage children to read by giving free books to their parents. 'That may work for upper middle-class kids,' she yelled, 'but giving these kids books, to my mind, how naive, when they are suffering depression, they're victims of drug dependency, family abuse!' It opened the way for Latham to tell the audience of his own childhood in a tough neighbourhood. 'You never, ever use disadvantage as an excuse for irresponsible or bad behaviour,' he said. Keri-lea Menzies fumed out of the hall, yelling to Latham, 'You're a silver spooner—go home and have a three-course dinner!'

The clash highlighted Latham's credo of self-help, ambition and personal responsibility against Labor's traditional role as the giver of big-dollar safety nets for the poor and troubled. He was not about trying to find a way of agreeing with dissenters, but nor would he refuse to talk with them. His Coalition opponents could hardly attack him for promoting individual responsibility. The audience—mainly middle-aged and beyond—seemed to agree with Latham and some jeered Keri-lea. She was the focus of television news coverage that night—and in the next day's newspapers. Latham's minders were more than pleased. They had been troubled earlier when some of the reporters on the bus suggested that pro-Labor questioners had been planted in the audience. Now the minders joked that Keri-lea Menzies was their best plant yet. That night a more relaxed Latham pulled on his jeans and joined the travelling media for pizza.

Yet, the incident re-ran a nagging question in the minds of long-term Latham watchers on the bus: how did he really feel about those who could never climb the ladder of opportunity he liked to describe? Were they the slackers his mother had so loathed? What solutions did he have for people who'd arrived at no hope through little fault of their own? Latham was a man who liked to label those who didn't work. It would lead to conflict with his staff.

On the afternoon Latham was elected leader, Tim Gartrell, Labor's national secretary, visited him at Parliament House. Gartrell knew he'd stand or fall in his position as the party organisation's chief on the preparedness and quality of the election campaign he would direct. Like many others in the party, Gartrell was surprised at the result of the leadership ballot. There had been an expectation within Labor's Canberra headquarters that Beazley would win. To them, it seemed he had greater party factional and union backing. He was a man they well knew. From their frequent private polling on Beazley, they were sure he was well liked and seen as experienced. But they also knew there were questions in voters' minds about Beazley's capacity to be prime minister.

Latham was much less familiar to headquarters staff and the polling that had been done on voter attitudes toward him showed he was largely unknown. Gartrell and Latham talked about the possible timing of an election and how to deal with politically charged issues, such as Labor's policy on boat people, at the party's January national conference. Gartrell had decided to be direct with Latham, although he knew the new leader could be testy. Knowing that Latham was a possible leadership contender, in the months before the ballot Gartrell had thrown Latham's name up for feedback in Labor's focus group research. He now told Latham that the research—albeit limited—showed he had a serious problem with women voters. Many didn't like him. They thought he was aggressive and crude. His earthy language had come up time and time again as a negative. He'd once called Howard an arse licker and had used Sydney Westie language when he described the Liberal Party as a conga line of suckholes. He'd talked about muscling up to the government in Parliament and he had flattened a Sydney taxi driver with a crash tackle that broke the driver's arm. It was no wonder Latham made many women apprehensive.

Intuitively, Latham had come part way to the recognition that women voters presented a problem. He'd always known, because of his mix of aggression and sometimes choice language, that he was more popular with men. That was why he had promised no more crudities at his first press conference. Gartrell now told him that it was urgent that he start to do more to appeal to women voters. Women made up the majority of swinging voters and therefore some early policies that favoured families should be developed and announced. Latham took Gartrell's words with good grace. He didn't contest what he was being told. It was a relief for Gartrell, who felt that Latham was ready to be much more inclusive and willing to take advice than he'd been as shadow Treasurer.

The pair had had spats then. Gartrell's sense that a calm had come over Latham once he became leader was shared by the Canberra MP and Labor frontbencher Bob McMullan. McMullan believed that Latham relaxed into the leadership, having got what he wanted, whereas Simon Crean never did, remaining frenetic during his time as leader.

The upshot of that conversation soon came. School visits quickly became a big feature on Latham's bus tours. He stressed the importance of early childhood reading, sitting on classroom floors with books in hand. Fatherhood had given him a familiarity with children's literature and Latham genuinely believed in the value of reading daily to his two young sons. The school visits were intended to show women that Latham was a caring, intelligent father who understood the chaos of raising kids. It worked. Labor's polling showed a spike in Latham's standing with female voters. When he took over as leader, only 26 per cent of women rated him as a potential prime minister. Through February, the proportion climbed to 34 per cent.

In Western Australia, Howard looked on and mimicked. Or his minders told him to. The pictures of a 64-year-old prime minister contorting into a squat on a floor reading to children looked thoroughly staged and awkward. It was enough for Labor to know that Howard was rattled by Latham's tactics. The press gallery reporters travelling with Howard dubbed his sweep through Western Australia the seniors tour. One of those journalists travelling with Howard was Latham's most fierce critic—the *Daily Telegraph*'s shrill columnist, Piers Ackerman. Vexed by the largely favourable coverage the press gallery was giving Latham, Ackerman called the journalists tadpoles and said Latham had set a poor national example by allowing himself to be photographed riding unsecured in the back of a farm ute.

But others, such as the nationally respected Laurie Oakes, saw danger for Howard. Oakes wrote of Latham's first weeks as leader:

The new Labor leader is not proving the easy target the Coalition expected. He is not the one-dimensional figure they thought. No sooner had the caucus votes been counted than the foul-mouthed thug morphed into sensitive family man. The volatile politician with a short fuse suddenly developed the ability to absorb attacks and insults without responding.[1]

After his election to the Labor leadership in December, Latham had taken Janine and their two young boys, Isaac and Oliver, to her home town Perth for part of the Christmas holidays. Latham's mind was on the Labor Party national conference to be held at Sydney's Darling Harbour Convention Centre in late January. The new venue ended a long Labor tradition of trooping down to Hobart for conferences that were often boozy and raucous as delegates and the media played up far from home. The change had been forced by Labor's 2002 decision to double the number of conference delegates to 400—too many for Hobart's Wrest Point Casino.

The 2004 conference would be the unveiling of Labor's new leader in an election year. It would send early signs to many people about whether or not Latham was capable of leading his party and the country. It needed to go well. Behind the scenes, the organisers were unusually jittery. Tim Gartrell fretted that with a new leader, a new venue and twice the number of delegates the party might have created a volatile mix. He believed there were three issues upon which the conference could founder: free trade, Labor's preferred site for a second Sydney airport and—most likely and damaging of all—Labor's continued support for the Howard government's mandatory detention of suspected illegal immigrants.

The refugee issue was deeply troubling for the Labor Party. Beazley's handling of the *Tampa* incident in 2001—when Howard had used troops to prevent a Norwegian freighter from unloading rescued asylum seekers on Australian territory—had appalled Latham. Howard's stand not only received wide public support, but it won him a third term in office. Latham believed the issue blew up in Labor's face because of Beazley's failure to have a clear-cut asylum-seeker policy. He believed Labor had been wishy-washy on the refugee issue, trying to be too many things to too many people. He also believed it was another demonstration of the failure of Beazley's small target policy strategy. As a western Sydney MP, he knew the depth of support Howard's policy had. Ranged against him would be the Labor Party's new president, Carmen Lawrence, a passionate opponent of mandatory detention, who resigned in disgust from Labor's frontbench in late 2002 accusing her colleagues of being gutless on refugees. And supporting Lawrence would be Labor's affectionately regarded former president, Barry Jones, a man with an enlarged social conscience. Both intended to support the well-organised and articulate ginger group, Labor for Refugees. This group wanted Australia's remote, prison-like detention centres shut and replaced with a system of community-based accommodation and periodic reporting for asylum seekers. They also wanted an end to the Temporary Protection Visa system which denied most government social services to people whose refugee claims had been successful.

Such a policy shift would have been difficult for the Labor Party, which had introduced mandatory detention when Bob Hawke was prime minister. No other issue so exposed the differences between Labor's blue collar, traditional working-class supporters and its educated, liberal constituency. To soften the policy might well lessen the leakage of this latter group of supporters to the Greens. But it would also hand John Howard —again—the incendiary border-protection wedge against Labor that had served him so well when the *Tampa* sailed into view.

On the last day of Parliament in 2003, the new Labor leader sought out the Western Australian MP, one-time lawyer and university lecturer Stephen Smith, who had been an energetic supporter of Kim Beazley. Smith, in his late 40s, had taken himself off to the backbench after Beazley's failure to oust Crean. It was a waste of talent. Smith had many qualities the Labor frontbench needed, not the least of which was a fastidious attention to detail. Even though he had been one of those castigated by Latham for destabilising Crean, Latham now told Smith he wanted him back. He offered him the immigration portfolio. He wanted Smith to use his low-key negotiating skills to head off a damaging confrontation on the conference floor between both sides of the asylum-seeker debate. Smith's Western Australian roots were also in Latham's mind. Smith and Lawrence—also a Western Australian—had known one another for a long time. Smith decided to sound Lawrence out to see if there was any room for movement.

When Latham was in Perth for Christmas, Smith took him to a Fremantle cafe. They lunched with Lawrence over bowls of mussels. She wanted to gauge how far Latham and Smith were prepared to go and sternly set out her view that mandatory detention was barbaric, that Temporary Protection Visas should be abolished and that Christmas Island should be restored to Australia's migration zone. The Howard government had deemed this little part of Australia to be not of Australia if boat people landed there, which they frequently did. It was the lawyer's fix to stop them claiming asylum.

Lawrence argued that changing the asylum-seeker policy was morally the right thing to do and that the electoral backlash from such a change would not be nearly as fearful as Latham and Smith believed. But her lunch companions thought it too hard for Labor to retreat. They believed the party would not withstand the electoral fallout. In early January, Smith and Lawrence met again for lunch—this time at a Subiaco restaurant. They talked for two hours but nothing changed. As Smith walked out, his phone rang. It was Latham's office wanting to know how lunch went. 'No problems,' said Smith. 'We haven't agreed on anything.'

There would now be a huge clash on migration at the conference. The problem was how to stem the blood on the carpet at Darling Harbour. Smith flew to Sydney and briefed his shadow cabinet colleagues on the asylum-seeker policy he believed the party should adopt. It kept the basics of the Howard government's mandatory detention policy but with the proviso that children be freed from the detention centres and placed in the community. It also set a twelve month deadline for the determination of applications to stay in Australia. The proposed policy also reduced the length of time that successful asylum seekers were denied the full range of government social services and benefits. The Howard government's policy of holding suspected illegal migrants at hastily built and remote holding places around the Pacific would be abandoned. To pre-empt the conference, Latham and Smith announced much of the policy a week before—a tactic designed to take some of the heat out of the coming debate.

But their move did not head off an impassioned attack from the conference floor led by Lawrence and Barry Jones, who electrified delegates when he declared that the war-time Swedish hero Raul Wallenberg, who saved many hundreds of Jews from the Nazis, would be declared a people smuggler in this day and age. Lawrence said the conference was being asked to cast aside a truly Labor policy for a facsimile of Howard's policy. Frontbencher Lindsay Tanner supported Labor for Refugees and, in a quavering voice, told the story of a Chinese boyhood friend who would often go to the local Catholic Church in country Victoria where Tanner lived, weeping and asking God why he'd been born with yellow skin. He later fled to Hong Kong and became a multi-millionaire.

The Labor premiers, NSW's Bob Carr and WA's Geoff Gallop, backed the Latham–Smith policy. Carr was loudly heckled from the conference floor when he said that public opinion was paramount. 'The Australian people cannot be ignored and their sentiment cannot be dismissed,' he said. 'To imagine it's a different view and to craft policy accordingly is to give John Howard the Labor Party policy he is waiting for.' Eventually, after an hour and a half of debate, the Latham plan was adopted by 226 votes to 166. The Right and Centre factions had combined against the Left to defeat Lawrence's position. When it was over Latham appealed for unity. It was a victory the new leader had to have. Certainly, some right-wing delegates who had been intending to support Lawrence and Jones had been bludgeoned by factional bosses and changed their minds. Nevertheless, the debate was an inspiring spectacle in an age of nauseating stage management. The passions were real and were allowed to flow.

Latham had begun work on his speech to the conference over Christmas. He wrote most of it himself. He knew it would be the speech that would be seen as the starting gun to the election year. And it would be his first big speech since becoming leader. He would be judged by many. He wanted it to be authentically his own work and of his own story. And a platform that would be right for Australia.

He walked into the convention centre holding Janine's hand to the sound of the prematurely dead rock star Michael Hutchence singing the INXS hit, 'New Sensation'. The song was a stirring, edgy choice. It might have caused some to wonder if Latham would also be a brilliant star who would tear across the universe and disintegrate before his time.

Latham opened by saying he didn't believe in opposition for opposition's sake. He sprinkled optimism through his lines— as if to accentuate a tired defensiveness in Howard. His opponents campaigned on fear, Labor on opportunity, he said. He told delegates they lived in a big country—in size, spirit and character—and their task was to be bigger than Howard. He offered touchstones for the ordinary and won applause with his line that he didn't want Australians to have to make the false choice between being a good parent and being a good employee. He told his own story of childhood and youth in

Green Valley, of his family's struggle and troubles at home. He said he'd lived the ladder of opportunity. He also acknowledged the importance of the alliance with the US, but stressed an independent Australia. He ended by saying the people's worries were the Labor Party's worries.

The delegates cheered and stamped. A cynic would say that was what they were supposed to do; that they always did. But there was something real. It seemed the Labor Party sensed the way back. Latham held out the new hope that the Labor Party under him had a real chance of beating Howard.

The government did land a blow on the Labor leader, however, when it uncovered early drafts of Latham's speech. It was an embarrassment. A hurt and angry Latham ranted to his staff. The draft showed he'd dropped pledges to say 'sorry' to Aboriginal Australians, and to work more closely with the trade unions. The draft also contained a promise to cut higher marginal tax rates.

The leak also revealed one sentence in Latham's drafts that caused the most angst in his office. Latham had originally wanted to use the word 'bludgers' in the line: 'When I was young, my mum used to tell me there were two types of people in our street—the slackers and the hard workers.' Some of his staff were horrified. They told him they were concerned that many people on benefits were in that situation through no fault of their own—such as the sick or those laid off. They saw the term as a slight to people on welfare. He changed the description to 'slackers'.

It turned out Latham's office was inadvertently responsible for the leak. A young volunteer had activated a computer program that makes a log of changes to draft documents. When the final speech was emailed out, the log of changes was still embedded. Latham rounded upon his senior staff for allowing a volunteer worker to electronically distribute the speech.

In Canberra, Howard called in the press to denounce Latham's conference speech. Most reports suggested Latham's gathering momentum had surprised Howard and that explained the prime minister's rare press conference at The Lodge. Howard denied it, but very soon events would suggest otherwise.

In 2003, while Simon Crean was leader, the Tasmanian Labor senator Nick Sherry had privately proposed within the party that Labor should abolish the hugely generous and long controversial parliamentary superannuation scheme. Under the scheme parliamentarians received an employer contribution that was, effectively, worth about 55 per cent of their salary. This was about seven times more generous than the standard for most Australian workers. The Sherry plan didn't make it into announced Labor policy under Crean but the then shadow Treasurer, Mark Latham, was impressed with the idea. He believed the public was cynical about politicians because of double standards and the super issue was the biggest double standard of all. There was no defence for it. Once he became leader, Latham decided to polish up the plan, take it to shadow cabinet and run with it.

On the first sitting day of Parliament in 2004 Latham announced the new policy. While he could not apply the changes to the super packages of existing members of parliament, Latham said that if he became prime minister, he would cut his super entitlement to the level of cabinet minister—meaning he would forgo at least $500 000 in future benefits. It wrong-footed Howard and the Coalition, who had been basking in the overnight signing in Washington of the Free Trade Agreement with the United States, which they clearly expected would dominate the first week of Parliament.

Despite a Newspoll showing Latham had made great gains for Labor over January, Howard was cocky. He was gearing up to attack Latham over his refusal to back the Free Trade Agreement. But Howard was curiously noncommittal over Latham's plan to cut politicians' super, telling reporters that he'd make no comment until he'd analysed all of what Latham had said. It was curious because Howard and his Treasurer, Peter Costello, had both firmly backed the politicians' scheme in the previous months. Indeed, Costello had again defended the scheme after Latham's announcement, saying publicly that Parliament ought to be doing things that would improve the quality of MPs and Latham's plan went against that. His Liberal frontbench colleague Tony Abbott said Latham was running a populist campaign based on envy. Howard's caution, however, wasn't shared by the young NSW Liberal leader John Brogden, who countered Costello and Abbott by applauding Latham's move. The *Sydney Morning Herald* splashed the Brogden story all over its front page. The *Herald*'s grunt fired up talkback radio the next day. The genie was well out of the bottle. The super issue, because it was so harnessed to the public's frustration with grasping politicians, blitzed the government's efforts to dominate the first week of Parliament.

Late on the afternoon of Thursday 12 February, after two sickly days for the Coalition in a hot and sticky Canberra, Howard called a snap cabinet meeting followed by a meeting of Coalition MPs. The prime minister said he was going to match Latham's plan. The Liberal politicians called in to endorse Howard's move were stunned. Some were greatly angered. It was a highly emotional party room meeting. Howard's authority was directly confronted in a way that had not happened since he became prime minister. And what was said to him was well leaked. The next day's *Australian Financial Review* reported that Howard was labelled craven and blinking by his own parliamentary colleagues. The Liberal member for Mackellar, Bronwyn Bishop, told Howard: 'We will never satisfy the public, they will never thank us for this. The public are insatiable when it comes to politicians, they'll take everything away from us if we give in.' Queensland Liberal Senator George Brandis said: 'You're facing Mr Latham and you're blinking.'

Howard called a press conference so as to make that night's 6 pm news. He told journalists assembled in the courtyard outside his parliamentary office: 'Rather than this thing drift on for months, I've decided to act immediately to get it off the agenda as a partisan political issue so that we can have a focus on issues that are really important.' Howard had been far blunter in the Liberals' party room, where he said it was an absolute political necessity to kill off the issue which had overwhelmed the week.

The backdown was most galling for Peter Costello and Tony Abbott, who had both publicly defended the existing scheme. Just that day in Question Time, Costello had been haranguing Latham as a flip-flop who made his head spin. Costello said nothing in public after Howard's backdown but *The Bulletin*'s Tony Wright later wrote a telling piece about an 'unprintable' tirade unleashed by Costello at Canberra airport to fellow Liberals that night. The decision also led to a fresh round of unhelpful speculation within the Liberal Party and the media about Costello succeeding Howard. Costello aided it. For days he pointedly refused to rule out a challenge. It was a terrible start for Howard at the beginning of the election year.

Publicly, Latham was restrained, saying he welcomed Howard's adoption of Labor policy. Privately he was elated. He had believed Howard would dig in on the super issue after Costello and Abbott had defended the existing scheme. When Howard backflipped, it became apparent to Latham that the cabinet was far more disorganised that he thought. Latham felt the prime minister's decision had given his leadership of the Labor Party a legitimacy it didn't have before that week began. The Opposition had, in effect, got its own policy through the Parliament. It filled Latham with confidence. The press gallery lauded him.

Three weeks later the *Sydney Morning Herald* ran a front page story which said Latham was now the most popular opposition leader since Bob Hawke. Based upon its ACNielsen poll, Labor would have crushed Howard's government if an election had been held in early March.

The false dawn was on the rise.

Chapter 5

Autumn in Iraq

A FEW HOURS AFTER HE WAS ELECTED LABOR LEADER IN December 2003, Mark Latham told leadership rival, Queensland MP and former diplomat Kevin Rudd, that he wanted him to stay on as shadow minister for Foreign Affairs. Relations between the pair, though cordial, were not particularly warm. The urbane and neat Rudd believed Latham had been cool toward him because Rudd's own fatherless rise out of childhood impoverishment in rural Queensland rivalled Latham's boyhood story.

When Rudd agreed to stay, Latham told him he was concerned about the Opposition's relationship with the United States. The Labor leader had famously dismissed George Bush as the most dangerous and incompetent US president in living memory, had labelled John Howard an arse-licker for being too ready to cosy up to the United States and had called Howard's Liberal Party a conga line of suckholes. Latham now recognised he needed to do some fence mending. Rudd set to work, arranging a meeting between Latham and the US Ambassador to Australia, Tom Schieffer, a Texas lawyer and close business associate of the president, who had been in partnership with Bush as an owner of the Texas Rangers baseball team.

Two days later Rudd was back in Latham's office. Schieffer had arrived at Parliament House and was on his way to see Latham. Rudd was running a last minute rehearsal on how Latham should play the ambassador, who was about to come through the door. Rudd knew that Schieffer—although close to Bush—was a Democrat and he advised Latham to speak of his own admiration for the former Democrat president, Texan Lyndon Johnson. Then Rudd cast a last look around the small room they were in—Latham had not yet moved into the larger Opposition leader's office. His jaw dropped. On the wall behind Latham's chair was a large, unpublished colour cartoon by the artist Bill Leak. It showed John Howard up the backside of a bent over and delighted George Bush. Horrified, Rudd lunged for the offending picture and shoved it behind a cabinet. Schieffer walked in a moment later.

Rudd could do nothing about the other piece of offending imagery that day. An eager young Latham staffer had positioned a US flag in the large Labor caucus room where a throng of reporters and camera crews had gathered for a post-meeting press conference to be given by Latham. Schieffer was not there. Latham did not see the flag but Rudd did and he immediately recognised that Latham would be roundly pilloried for doing his own bit of arse-licking—allowing the Stars and Stripes into the sovereign territory of the Labor caucus room didn't say a lot for the independent foreign policy mapped out by Latham. Rudd thought about moving the flag but realised, given the presence of journalists, that this would create its own diplomatic furore. He considered standing in front of it, but it was too late. Latham had to admit to Kerry O'Brien on the *7.30 Report* that night that he'd dropped a clanger. He lamely tried to defend the flag's presence by saying that John Curtin, the long-dead Labor wartime prime minister whose picture hung on the caucus room wall, would have looked down approvingly on the Stars and Stripes.

That Rudd had wanted to avoid the ambassador seeing

the Bush cartoon and the Australian public seeing the flag says much about the delicacy of Labor's relationship with the United States post the invasion of Iraq. Labor didn't want to give any further offence to the United States, but neither did it want to be seen giving a cringing apology. Serious trouble lay ahead.

On 23 March 2004, during an interview with Sydney radio broadcaster Mike Carlton, Latham dropped a bombshell that would goad Howard, enrage the United States and stun even some in his own party. If Labor won the election, Latham said, he would have Australian troops stationed in Iraq home by Christmas. Given the competing claims that would follow about whether or not Latham went beyond what had been agreed by the shadow cabinet, it is worth recording the detail of the interview. After Latham said the war in Iraq had made Australia more vulnerable to terrorist attack, Carlton put an obvious question:

Carlton: Should we then bring our troops home?

Latham: Well, we should. When they finish their responsibilities for the post-war reconstruction.

Carlton: But that may be ten years away. How long do they stay?

Latham: We believe we have a responsibility to rebuild that country and as soon as that responsibility is discharged, they should be back here. Hopefully that will be before the end of the year. Under a Labor government our strategy is to get them back as soon as that responsibility is discharged, and you have got a sovereign handover to a new Iraq government.

Carlton: You are being a bit wishy-washy there, leaving us a lot of room to move. How do you decide when they have discharged their responsibilities and bring them back?

Latham: Well, at the point of sovereign handover to a new government in Iraq. As you say, there is a timetable [for sovereignty], a very tentative timetable, for the middle of the year. Things can go wrong, things can get pushed back awhile, but our intention is to ensure that once the responsibility is discharged and that is at the time of the handover to the new sovereign government in Iraq, then Australian troops will come back under a Labor government.

Having succeeded in tying Latham down on when he considered the job of Australian troops in Iraq over, Carlton wanted to firm up the deadline.

Carlton: And you would hope they would be home by Christmas?

Latham: Yes, well if that timetable of mid year is adhered to, then that would be the case. If a federal election is held this year, say the election was in September and there was a change of government, we would be hoping to have them back by Christmas, certainly.

The reaction was immediate, wide and savage. Latham had hit on an issue that would dominate Australian politics right through the coming winter. It set off shudders within the Labor Party and glee within the government, which saw within Latham's promise the political wedge, the point of difference it had been seeking to rein in the Labor juggernaut. Howard's Foreign Affairs minister Alexander Downer led the first charge against Latham, saying part of the task of Australian troops in Iraq was to protect Australian diplomats and other officials. If the troops left, so would they. Howard painted Latham as betraying Australian values, telling Parliament it was not the Australian way to cut and run. A trio of commentators from *The Australian*, Paul Kelly, Greg Sheridan and Christopher

Pearson, waded in against Latham. So did their counterparts in the Fairfax press, Greg Hywood and Gerard Henderson. Kelly said terrorists the world over would rejoice. Hywood dismissed Latham as a Sydney suburban politician out of his depth in high foreign policy issues. Ambassador Schieffer made a controversial intervention into Australian domestic issues by implying that Latham's stance invited more terrorism.

At the top of the Labor Party, Latham's position on the troops caused deep concern. He had taken on the Coalition over national security, territory that was owned, electorally, by Howard. Tim Gartrell, the party's federal secretary, had had no warning of what Latham would say in the Carlton interview. Had he been warned, he would have tried to talk Latham out of the promise to bring the troops home by Christmas. He would have brought in the Labor Party's wiser foreign policy heads, such as Kim Beazley and Kevin Rudd, to help. Gartrell's concerns only multiplied when he saw the results of Labor's internal polling on the issue in late April—focus groups designed to establish the public's reaction to Latham's promise showed mounting voter concern over damage to the Australian–United States alliance for which there was overwhelming public support. Gartrell told Latham about his worries and the private polling results. He stressed the importance of the US alliance in the public mind and his concern that Latham had left himself very little room to modify or abandon his promise if events forced a rethink.

The pledge to bring troops home had become a millstone for Latham and the Labor Party. It had been a distraction from Latham's attempts to cast himself as the positive, optimistic young leader who stood in clear contrast to Howard. Gartrell feared it would add to what he correctly detected to be the beginnings of a subtle but deadly campaign by Howard to portray Latham as not ready—yet—to be prime minister. Howard was careful not to say Latham was not fit to lead, just that now was not the time. Gartrell believed such a campaign would be poisonous for Latham because it gave those who were becoming sympathetic to him an excuse not to vote for him this time around. And the manner of Latham's announcement gave oxygen to such a campaign. While it was true that Latham had been thinking for some time about delivering the commitment, the way he had just dropped it into a radio interview gave the appearance that it was a policy made on the run. That was certainly the way most of the Canberra press gallery viewed it.

There was also evidence that shadow cabinet ructions caused by Latham's promise were behind a damaging leak. The influential Channel Nine political correspondent and *Bulletin* columnist, Laurie Oakes, called Tim Gartrell at his home on Sunday 18 April, and told the Labor Party chief he knew the party had been conducting private polling on Latham's promise. Gartrell was surprised. He'd only just seen the results of the polling himself. Three days later, Oakes's column in *The Bulletin* exposed Labor's internal polling and its conclusion that there was overwhelming public support for the alliance with the US. Gartrell suspected a senior member of the shadow cabinet who had a deep interest in Iraq, who disagreed with Latham and who had been shown the polling had leaked the results to Oakes. A turning point had been reached, Gartrell believed. The Latham honeymoon was over. Hostilities within the party had begun.

On the night of Wednesday 7 April, Latham delivered his first big speech on foreign policy to Sydney's Lowy Institute for International Policy, a think-tank founded by the Westfield shopping centre magnate Frank Lowy. Many of the heavy hitters in the foreign affairs club were present. It was a thoughtful, if cautious, speech that recommitted Labor to the three big constants of Australian foreign policy: the alliance with the United States, the United Nations and strong relations with Asia. Latham went on in his speech to say how his approach to each would differ from that of the Howard government. On the most important component—the alliance with the United States—Latham said he would jettison the Coalition's approach of following the US into wars to buy insurance for Australia. Instead, Labor would seek what Latham called a more equal partnership that emphasised foremost Australia's own security.

The *Sydney Morning Herald's* Peter Hartcher, who covered the last of the Keating years in Canberra and then went on to distinguish himself as a foreign correspondent in Japan and the US, best caught Latham's drift. Latham, he later wrote, passed the test of articulating a credible foreign policy. But some of his ideas and key lines were straight out of the Paul Keating book of foreign policy. Oakes, too, remarked in *The Bulletin* on the apparent influence of Keating. Later, Keating's closest advisor in his Canberra years—Dr Don Russell, whom he appointed Australian Ambassador to Washington—wrote that Latham's speech was a return to the policies of the Hawke–Keating years.

To many, it begged the question of whether Keating influenced Latham's decision to bring the troops home early. Keating never said, nor did Latham. But Keating did make a sudden, sharp intervention in July after US deputy secretary of State, Richard Armitage, claimed the Labor Party was split down the middle on the troops home policy. On a Sydney to Canberra flight in early July, Keating read of Armitage's attack in the *Sydney Morning Herald*. Incensed, he borrowed a pen from the stranger in the seat beside him and drafted a statement. It was typically combative Keating: 'The [Labor] Party will not be thugged by US officials. In my own experience of Presidents Bush [Snr] and Clinton, no behaviour of this kind towards what the US might regard as a client state, was ever contemplated or attempted.' Keating appeared to telegraph his own support for the troops home policy when he added that there was no division in the Labor Party on the Iraq policy.

Whether or not Keating was an influence on Latham's pledge, Simon Crean and Kevin Rudd certainly were. But not because they'd urged Latham to bring the troops home. A powerful influence on his commitment was his fear of the past—not the future. Latham had been frustrated by Simon Crean's caveat-ridden positions on Australia's involvement in Iraq before the war began.

From early 2002, when it became apparent the United States would probably invade, through to the invasion itself, Crean and the Labor Party contorted themselves into a policy knot. In Crean's earliest official position—in April 2002—he was open to supporting an invasion if Iraq could be directly linked to the September 11 attacks in the United States the year before. Labor would also need evidence, he said, that Iraq was supplying weapons of mass destruction to terrorists. And even if Labor were to support the invasion it would permit no military involvement beyond intelligence co-operation and logistical support. There would be no Australian combatants. However, by September Crean had abandoned this position in favour of supporting the use of Australian forces, specifically the SAS, in Iraq. He explained the change by saying the SAS was finishing its tour in Afghanistan and would be available. The Labor position seemed even more confusing when Crean declined to rule out supporting a unilateral strike on Iraq, despite Labor saying it was insistent that the invasion receive United Nations backing. Labor's former Foreign Affairs spokesman, Laurie Brereton, broke ranks in exasperation with the party's various positions and declared on the eve of war in 2003 that Labor should not support the invasion under any circumstances, including with a United Nations mandate.

Crean was at his clearest just as the invasion—without United Nations backing—was about to start. On a hot Sydney Thursday in late January 2003, he went to Sydney's Garden Island naval dockyard to make a farewell speech to the 350 troops heading to Iraq aboard the heavy transporter, HMAS

Kanimbla. In a brave and controversial speech he told them, 'I don't want to mince my words because I don't believe you should be going'. No Australian leader since Arthur Calwell during the Vietnam War had openly opposed a military deployment and none had ever said so to departing troops.

Latham privately rued the fact that Labor's position on Iraq had only become clear to the public on the threshold of war. He blamed Rudd as much as Crean because Rudd was the Labor leader's main advisor. Latham believed Labor had suffered because for a year it had been in the vacillating middle on Iraq. In his mind, the Greens were at one extreme in opposing any war and Howard at the other. Labor was somewhere in between and fighting on two flanks. It was under fire from both the war's opponents and from its supporters. He believed people felt so passionately about Iraq that the Labor Party had to be clearly seen as being either for the war or against the war. Latham determined that if he became leader, the party would not be caught again.

In the weeks following his elevation to the leadership, Latham began to steer Labor towards a firmer position on the withdrawal of Australian forces from Iraq. He believed that Greens leader Bob Brown would begin demanding that Australian troops be brought home and that Labor would be caught without a firm timetable. In Latham's view, he needed to set one. He also anticipated a series of flare-ups in Iraq that would put further pressure on Labor from opponents of Australia's involvement in the war. But most of all it was a conversation he had back in early January that would push him into his promise to bring the troops home for Christmas.

On Monday 5 January 2004, a trim, tall man in his late 50s left Canberra in the early afternoon and drove up the Hume Highway to Sydney. Senior public servant Ron Bonighton's caution, discretion and obsession with detail invite comparisons with

John le Carré's London spymaster, George Smiley, as do his reserved good manners, his glasses and greying hair. Few outsiders know Bonighton is the top spy master in the Department of Defence where he serves as a deputy secretary. This was his first day back at work after Christmas holidays.

Bonighton turned off the highway at Ingleburn in Sydney's far south-west and pulled up outside Mark Latham's electorate office. He was going to give Latham a secret briefing on the role of Australia's military intelligence services. It was a privilege accorded to every new federal Opposition leader. Bonighton had been in Australia's intelligence services since graduating from Melbourne University in the late 1960s. He'd worked in Washington as Australia's liaison officer at the United States' National Security Agency and had headed the Defence Signals Directorate in Canberra—an electronic eavesdropping agency —before taking overall charge of defence intelligence. No one was better qualified to give the new leader of the Opposition a briefing.

It should have been a routine meeting to provide Latham with an overview of the agencies without going into operational matters. Few people knew that this meeting was taking place. However, two months later, just as Bonighton was about to be presented with an Order of Australia for services to Australian intelligence gathering, the January meeting exploded into the public arena. Latham and Bonighton would have sharply different recollections about what was said.

The meeting would not have come to light but for a muddleheaded taunt at Latham from Howard's Foreign Minister Alexander Downer tossed across the floor of the Parliament in late March. Labelling Latham's policy to bring the troops home from Iraq by Christmas as policy on the run, Downer added: 'Get a briefing, understand what the issues are and then work out what you want to do.' However, as Latham later revealed at a press conference, he had indeed had briefings, not only from Bonighton, but also by the director general of Australia's overseas spying agency, the Australian Secret Intelligence Service (ASIS).

Howard went into protection mode and obtained letters from the Department of Foreign Affairs, from Bonighton and from ASIS. Foreign Affairs said it had never briefed Latham on Iraq. ASIS said Iraq had not been mentioned in its briefing to Latham. But it was Bonighton's letter that proved the most controversial. He assured the government he had not discussed strategic or policy matters relating to Iraq with Latham. He said he'd mentioned Iraq only when giving examples of the kinds of intelligence support provided to Australian forces. According to Howard, Bonighton had made no reference to Iraq in his written record of his meeting with Latham.

This ran counter to Latham's recollection of what had been said but the Opposition leader was bound by strict security rules that prevented him revealing any details of the briefing. It can now be said, however, that on Latham's recollection, Bonighton convinced him during the hour or so they met why no weapons of mass destruction (WMD) would be found in Iraq: they did not exist. Latham was astounded given that Iraq's possession of such weapons had been the central plank in the decision by the United States, the United Kingdom and Australia to go to war. The Opposition leader concluded that the Iraq adventure was a fiasco and the sooner Australian troops came home, the better.

Latham did not know it then, but Bonighton had reason to know better than most in the Department of Defence the status of Saddam's WMDs. He was overseeing the activities of about fifteen Australian analysts and technical experts who were part of the Iraq Survey Group, the international body whose task it was to find and destroy Iraq's weapons of mass destruction. When Latham later learned of Bonighton's role, it only reinforced his view that his policy to pull out of Iraq was the right one.

It fell to Kevin Rudd to do much of the heavy lifting in publicly defending and explaining Latham's Christmas deadline. Rudd strained under the pressure. Suspicion that he was having to defend a policy about which he had not been properly consulted was heightened when Rudd was grilled by ABC-TV's Tony Jones on *Lateline* on 29 March 2004. Rudd said he and Latham had been 'discussing' setting a Christmas deadline for the withdrawal before Latham's announcement to Carlton.

> Jones: So you knew several weeks ago that Mark Latham planned to come out and say 'troops home by Christmas', did you?
>
> Rudd: I can't pinpoint any particular time as far as that's concerned, all I know is Mark and I had been discussing it for some time.
>
> Jones: The very line we are talking about—'troops home by Christmas'—you knew about that?
>
> Rudd: We'd been discussing it for some time.

At no time in his interview with Jones did Rudd say he knew in advance that Latham would make the promise. Rudd knew he could have left Latham marooned on this point. Instead, he decided he would shield Latham but would not lie. It was a delicate balancing act. Rudd, because of his background in Foreign Affairs, has a close knowledge of the United Nations' Iraq resolutions and the legal situation of the occupying powers. He was able to overwhelm most interviewers. He knew Latham was fighting on territory that was foreign to him and, in his own mind, he had entered the political trenches alongside Latham. They toughed it out and, later, Rudd came to believe that for the first time Latham realised he could rely on him.

Rudd had been caught out by Latham's promise to bring

the troops home. It can now be said that Rudd went to great lengths to urge Latham not to do it. A week before Latham made the announcement, Rudd had been interviewed on *Lateline*, also by Tony Jones, about the impact of Spain's involvement in Iraq, the terrible bombing by suspected local affiliates of al-Qaeda of two Madrid railway stations in which more than 200 people had been killed and the Spanish election result. The bombing turned victory away from Spain's ruling Conservatives and into the hands of the Socialists, who were against Spain's involvement in Iraq. Terrorism had influenced the election outcome.

Latham was at his Sydney home watching Rudd's 15 March interview on *Lateline*. The key question came toward the end when Jones asked if a Labor government would immediately bring Australian troops home from Iraq.

Rudd: Well Tony, nice try. You're trying to verbal me into a position, all I am saying . . .

Jones: I'm trying to actually hear a position from you because there isn't one on your party platform.

Rudd: Well, this is a fluid operational environment. You know that as well as I do. We actually, unlike the government, have argued a consistent, principled position, under international law, the Fourth Geneva Convention, which says, despite the fact we didn't like the government going in as part of the invasion force into Iraq, now that that's happened, we have obligations to look after the Iraqi people, together with the UK, the US, Poland and Spain.

It was a detailed, if long-winded answer. But Latham didn't like it. He called Rudd and left a message on his mobile phone saying he wanted to toughen up and sharpen Labor's policy on Iraq. Latham said he intended saying in a radio interview the next morning that, if elected prime minister, he'd bring Australian troops home by Christmas. He casually told his Foreign Affairs spokesman to call him if he wanted to discuss it.

By the time Rudd retrieved Latham's message it was well after 11 pm. Rudd desperately wanted to persuade the Labor leader not to set the Christmas deadline. But Latham had switched his phone off. So Rudd, ever careful to cover all points in an argument, left three long voicemail messages for Latham in which he expressed his opposition to Latham's plan and his reasons. In a nutshell his argument was that Australia had an obligation to help rebuild Iraq and that a withdrawal announcement by Latham would almost certainly wreck the improvement in relations between the Labor Party and the Bush administration that Latham had wanted.

The next day Latham advised Rudd he had rethought his proposal and would not make an announcement about withdrawing from Iraq.

Rudd then flew out to Kabul relieved at having changed Latham's mind. He later told senior colleagues what had happened. Rudd returned to Canberra a week later. The next day Latham announced to Mike Carlton that a Labor government would bring Australia's Iraq contingent home by Christmas. All of the fallout that Rudd had predicted quickly eventuated. Rudd was infuriated.

Many in the Labor Party saw Latham's position on Iraq as leaving him dangerously exposed on foreign policy and national security. Laurie Brereton and John Faulkner went to Latham's great rival for the leadership, Kim Beazley. Their mission was to persuade the former party leader to agree to come into Latham's shadow cabinet in a senior national security portfolio. Beazley was noncommittal. He had a painful neurological condition, and wanted time to think about his future.

✧

Shortly before 3 am on 25 April 2004, a lone Royal Australian Air Force Hercules transport slipped into Iraqi airspace from the south-east and soon began a steep, fast descent into Baghdad airport. On the ground many of the Australian soldiers at Camp Victory, the Australian base, knew a ministerial visit was on the cards for their dawn service on ANZAC Day, but hardly anyone knew that their guest would be John Howard. When George Bush made his surprise visit to Baghdad in November 2003 for Thanksgiving celebrations with American troops, he was rewarded with an immediate lift in the polls. Howard doubtless expected the same.

The visit produced plenty of drama for the small group of journalists who had been taken along on the trip after swearing to strict secrecy until the prime minister was out of Baghdad. They had pictures of him in a flak-jacket aboard the darkened aircraft, playing two-up with troops on the ground, and the story of a dramatic, evasive climb out of Baghdad because of fears of a missile attack on the aircraft. Sydney's tabloid *Daily Telegraph* ran a huge front-page picture of John Howard at Baghdad's dawn service, head bowed and flanked by two soldiers, under the headline 'DIGGING IN'.

The Liberal Party minders were ecstatic. Latham, wisely, wished the prime minister a safe return and did not complain about the trip being a taxpayer-funded public relations stunt. Much of the informed commentary in the Australian media now raised the prospect that Latham had committed a grave error with his troop withdrawal promise. Laurie Oakes, writing in *The Bulletin*, said the Labor leader had saved Howard the trouble of finding another *Tampa*. Even the lobbyist Bruce Hawker, the architect of many successful Labor campaigns and a member of Latham's campaign strategy committee, fretted in his Sydney office about the hardening of attitudes against Latham's policy.

✧

Steve Lewis is an enthusiastic newspaperman in the Canberra press gallery. Irrepressibly cheery and a member of the gallery's songsters, The House Howlers, he worked for the *Australian Financial Review* before moving down the corridor to join Rupert Murdoch's empire as *The Australian*'s political correspondent. That was how he ended up in the White House Rose Garden on 3 June 2004. Lewis was in a throng of media covering a joint press conference to be given by George Bush and John Howard. It was Howard's sixth meeting with Bush in two years. But to call it a press conference was a long bow. After listening to verbose statements of praise from each leader to the other, the waiting journalists were permitted just four questions: two from the Americans and two from the Australians. An American reporter almost drowned out Lewis as he attempted to ask the last question, but Howard interjected and called for the man from *The Australian* to go ahead. Lewis had the question that Howard wanted answered, out loud, by George Bush: what signal would Mark Latham's promised Christmas withdrawal of troops send to the Iraqi people and other nations in the coalition that occupied Iraq?

To Lewis's amazement, Bush opened up and he and his colleagues had front page news for home. 'I think that would be disastrous,' the President said. 'It would be a disastrous decision for the leader of a great country like Australia to say, "We're pulling out." It would dispirit those people who love freedom in Iraq. It would say the Australian government doesn't see hope of a free and democratic society leading to a peaceful world. It would embolden the enemy who believe they can shake our will. See, they want to kill innocent life, because they think the Western world, the free world, is weak. That when times get tough, we will shirk our duty to those who long for freedom, and we'll leave. And I, anyway [to now yelling reporters]—no, you can't [ask] any more. Thank you all for coming.'

'Thank you,' echoed a beaming John Howard.

The leader of the free world had declared war on the leader of the Australian Labor Party. In Canberra, Latham issued a measured but resolute statement that gave no concessions to Bush. He said the Howard government had sent Australian troops to Iraq to find weapons of mass destruction that had never existed. Australia had, as a result, become a bigger terrorist target. Labor had not wanted the troops in Iraq in the first place, and they would be home by Christmas.

The Americans wheeled out more big guns. Over the next few weeks Australian journalists suddenly found themselves with ready access to US secretary of state Colin Powell, and his deputy Richard Armitage. Armitage, the bull-necked, broad-shouldered, raspy voiced US Naval Academy graduate and Vietnam War veteran, was the more menacing and outspoken of the two. He made clear that Latham's stance threatened the Free Trade Agreement with the United States and, most pointedly, he invited Australians to think about life without the defensive shield provided by their military alliance with the United States. Powell said that he agreed with his president that Australia's withdrawal would be a disaster. On the question of consequences, Powell was more circumspect, saying Australia would always be a close friend of the US. Nevertheless, the warning had been starkly laid out for the Labor Party. There would have to be changes to the plan to bring the troops home by Christmas. The consequence of not doing so would be increasing public concern in Australia about the future of the military alliance with the United States. Labor knew from its own polling that this would be electoral poison for Latham.

A week before Bush delivered his condemnation of Latham's policy, Kim Beazley made a little-reported speech to the Australian Institute of International Affairs in Canberra. Beazley didn't circulate his speech notes around the press gallery and the man he most wanted to hear what he had to say wasn't in the audience. But Beazley knew others would get the gist of his words to Mark Latham. Beazley's core message to his audience that night was that while the Howard government might be the ally the United States wanted, it was not the ally the United States needed. He said Australia should have intervened forcefully in mid 2002 when debate was raging in Washington between the hawks and the doves on the need to invade Iraq. Australia could have put a case then against invasion. The message he wanted Latham to hear was in the body of his speech: that Australia had an obligation to assist the United States, indeed honour demanded it. But that did not oblige Australia to simply trail every twist and turn the US made as a child would a parent.

Only a few people knew then that Beazley was coming under strong pressure from Labor's factional heavies, Laurie Brereton, Robert Ray and John Faulkner, to move into Latham's shadow ministry. They were convinced that Latham needed Beazley back in the inner circle to head off fears among voters that a Latham Labor government could not credibly deal with national security. Beazley had declined a shadow ministry position offered by Latham after Latham beat him in the December leadership ballot. Now, however, the battering from the United States was taking a toll. Public support for Latham was weakening, particularly among older voters who were most worried about the US alliance. Besides, none of Latham's shadow ministers dealing with national security had ever been in cabinet before. Beazley knew that two of the emissaries sent to his office—Faulkner and Brereton—were close and trusted colleagues of Latham's. He realised that Latham was well aware of the overtures being made to him.

Beazley had worked out that a sea change in Latham's approach to the US alliance was on. His Canberra speech could be read as the policy price of his agreeing to go into a Latham cabinet—most likely in the position he had occupied twenty years ago in the first Hawke government, as minister for Defence. He had vast experience in defence and foreign policy and a network of high-level contacts across Asia and, more importantly, in Washington.

But Beazley wasn't ready to say yes. He'd fallen ill in March with a condition called Schaltenbrand's Syndrome. Spinal fluid leaks from around the brain, balance is unstable and weariness sets in. Sufferers are forced to spend weeks on their backs. Even in the recovery stage, Beazley looked like a man who'd had a stroke and he wasn't sure he had the stamina to return to the frontbench. But by the time he boarded a flight home from the United States in June he'd decided he was well enough to tell Latham he'd join the shadow ministry.

The pair met in early July and Beazley accepted Latham's offer to take on the Defence portfolio. An announcement was made on 12 July and that night Latham gave a speech to the Australian Institute of International Affairs—the same body Beazley had addressed in late May. Indeed, it might have been the same speech. Beazley had great input into Latham's words, which were designed to put an end to the damaging US criticism of Labor's Iraq policy. Latham announced that a Labor government would dispatch a force to Iraq to protect the United Nations mission once Australian troops were withdrawn. And he would take advice on whether some Australian troops needed to remain in Iraq to protect Australian officials. His speech rang with the themes Beazley had set out in his own May speech: the United States was overwhelmingly a force for good but Australia had not given its ally the advice it needed on Iraq.

The following day, US ambassador Tom Schieffer confirmed a thaw in relations between the Bush administration and Latham. He welcomed Latham's speech and the return of Beazley, a man he said the United States could work with.

The cartoon of John Howard up the bum of George Bush never again saw the light of day in Latham's office.

Chapter 6

Under the Radar

MONTHS BEFORE THE ELECTION MARK LATHAM TOOK A solitary decision. He would not take on John Howard over the economy. It was Howard's fortress, territory Labor could never win. Unemployment was at a record low, interest rates were screwed down, there was real growth in wages and salaries, and Australia was entering its fifteenth year of consecutive economic growth. His imagination likened Howard to a fixed piece of artillery, unable to swing its gun at a moving target. If the target camped within Howard's range—its centre being the economy—then the prime minister would destroy it. Instead, Latham would provide a moving target and ratchet everyday, suburban families up the political agenda. He believed Howard had ignored what mattered to them. Besides, they were people Labor needed back.

'I just reached the conclusion,' he said in early July 2004, 'thinking about this, well here [the economy] is Howard's battlefield, I am not going to sit there and get blown away until election day.

'So what was the alternative, the relevant agenda that suited the Labor agenda of fairness and helping people? I reached the conclusion that Howard had spoken a lot about families but there were many things he could have done for families that he'd forgotten about like reading to kids, vaccinating children, policies on childhood obesity, baby care payments and the very obvious one, bulk billing. There is a whole range of issues where Howard talks about families but it's just rhetoric. It's not actual, relevant policy. Some of ours are big policies. Some are small but relevant to people such as reading to kids and banning junk food ads. But it's an important area to develop and it's an area which the Howard government had neglected. We are better off setting that agenda than taking Paul Kelly's advice and going and sitting on this firing field and watching myself get blown to bits.'[1] [The *Australian*'s Paul Kelly had written in January 2004 that Latham's failure to restate his support for the market economy and Labor's role as the champion of economic reform were conspicuous omissions that clouded Latham's economic stance.]

To help understand why Latham, who has been an enthusiastic supporter of the market economy's ability to grow and create jobs, would not contest Howard on the economy, it is necessary to look to the past. There, too, are to be found the reasons for his risky values election campaign, built around home, families, schools, work and the environment.

Around the time of the 2000 Olympic Games, Mark Latham and David Britton (a founder of the Labor-aligned firm of political lobbyists, Hawker Britton) went to dinner at the glittering end of town—Aria restaurant above Sydney's Circular Quay where views from the deep, leather seats swoop from the Opera House to the Harbour Bridge. Their guest was Dick Morris, the American political strategist who steered Bill Clinton into the governorship of Arkansas, and then into his second term in the White House. The Clintons considered Morris's strategies brilliant and creative, although, as Hillary

Clinton wrote in her memoir, he had the people skills of a porcupine and sometimes his advice was off the wall. Nevertheless, Latham was a fan. A big one. He'd read Morris's writing on strategy and, while he didn't agree with all of it, there was much that matched his own ideas.

A year earlier Morris had published *The New Prince*, a book that further catapulted his reputation in the United States as the political strategist for the times. It was inspired by the most famous guide to political strategy ever written, Niccolo Machiavelli's *The Prince*, published 500 years earlier.

Morris's book became essential reading for government staffers as Latham's political tactics and style unfolded early in 2004. There was much in it that mirrored Latham's methods: the raising of non-mainstream issues which leapt like wildfire between groups of voters and confused John Howard; Latham's reliance on issues—not style—to brand himself; the overwhelming emphasis on positive rather than negative messages; the elevation of one big, controversial issue (Iraq) that generated more enemies and alienated interest groups but which came to say a lot about Latham to a quizzical public.

While Latham, in the lead-up to the 2004 election, acknowledged that Morris was an influence in his thinking, the Labor leader had not spared his praise for the American strategist back in 1999 when he was a backbencher in exile. In an article he wrote for the *Australian Financial Review* in mid-1999, Latham said:

> Morris is the Machiavelli of our time. His success as a political consultant in the United States is now matched by his dazzling insights and advice in printed form. He makes the rest of us look like flim-flam on the atlas of public life.

Later in the same article, Latham supplied what could now pass as the modus operandi he would use once elected leader of the Labor Party:

The new prince of politics needs to base his work on a practical campaign of ideas, the small bricks of progress which build a more capable society. He shouldn't be scared of taking on vested interests and defining himself by the extreme rhetoric of his opponents. He shouldn't be afraid of 'cross-over' policies which address issues traditionally associated with the other side of politics . . . The true test of character in the new politics does not concern cheesy family photos or trumped-up stories about community service. It concerns issues and conviction.

From that very first bus trip on the highway north out of Sydney in February 2004, much of the war game that Latham had written about was put into practice. He stressed the need for parents to read often to their children. A small brick of progress. He confronted possibly the most loathed vested interest in the nation—politicians bent on keeping their overly generous retirement scheme. And he was not afraid to hijack causes traditionally owned by his political opponents. His defence at the Labor Party national conference of mandatory detention for asylum seekers was an example of the power of the cross-over politics about which he'd written.

It was guerrilla warfare. Latham bobbed up with bagfuls of homely fixes in and outside Parliament. Just when the government had mustered the information to confront him, he'd move fast to another battleground: the need for boys to have male mentors; curbs on the activities of political lobbyists; a pledge to live in just one taxpayer-funded house as prime minister; a promise to the elderly to slash dental waiting lists; a recognition of the loneliness of many people's lives; the yearning for a return to local issues by many women whose eyes glazed over, Latham said, when politicians spoke of macro economics and politics; curbs on spruikers phoning families at dinner time; doing something about the enormous salaries for corporate heads. The barrage was fathered by Latham's conviction that people had not lost interest in politics. They just wanted politics to be more relevant to their everyday lives, to things that they could touch, which touched them. He was flying beneath Howard's radar.

Latham illustrated his belief that many people had been made weary and numb by the way politicians talked about the economy when he exercised his right-of-reply in Parliament to the 2004 budget. Seen as an opportunity for the Opposition to lay out its economic policies, Latham confounded the media with an unconventional speech that gave scant details of his tax and family policy. Instead, he allowed his speech to be over-shadowed by an event he had orchestrated earlier that day with his Health spokeswoman, the Victorian MP and former lawyer Julia Gillard.

The pair had called a media conference in the Opposition's Parliament House party room. With them was a young mother, Jennifer Brooks, and her 15-month-old child, Bella, who had been diagnosed with pneumococcal disease. Gillard had been astounded to discover that Peter Costello's budget made no provision for funding the vaccination of children against this crippling disease, which can cause blindness, deafness and spinal problems. She had expected a budget allocation to be made because she knew the government had been in negotia-tions with drug companies. It appeared to have been dropped to save money.

Confident and articulate, Jennifer Brooks was a convincing reason for Latham's announcement that day that Labor would fund the vaccinations. She spoke through her tears of her love for Bella and the need for other children to be protected. Gillard's eyes misted over, too. So did some of the reporters'. The story was placed high up in that night's television news bulletins, overwhelming the government's efforts to sell its big budget tax cuts. The government was left scrambling to match Labor's promise. It pleaded that it was still negotiating with the drug companies. The television imagery of Latham going into bat for a mother and her infant with a life-threatening disease was powerful. The government was left looking churlish with its protests that it was still trying to screw a deal out of the drug companies. This was an issue that met Latham's test for relevance to peoples' lives.

But it wasn't just a matter of Labor's bigger heart. Beneath the soft pictures of little Bella Brooks was a hard strategy. And its originator was Dick Morris. He had named it, grandly, as triangulation. It could also be called the Third Way, the description most often used for Tony Blair's style of Labour government in Britain. The essence of Morris's theory was that political leaders should try to solve their opponents' problems. The solution would, ideally, be a third position—above the traditional positions of politics' opposing forces. And it would be one that highlighted the everyday concerns of ordinary people. Bella Brooks was its front. While the Howard government was in overdrive selling the benefits of a lavish budget that ran into tens of millions of dollars in new spending, Latham wanted to be seen on the side of a little girl who had missed out.

Such tactics flummoxed the Coalition. They caused the *Australian Financial Review*'s chief political correspondent, Laura Tingle, to write in late May: 'The Coalition has gone into the sort of panic-induced freefall you can only associate with a government that knows it is on its way out and has no idea of how to stop it.'

Another of Latham's tactics that Morris had pioneered was to steer clear of the economy. In fact, Morris devoted a chapter of his book to explaining why he believed American voters had shifted from economic concerns to social-values issues. He wrote:

A majority of our countrymen understand that an increase in their disposable income is not going to solve the major problems in their lives. Crime, pollution and its health impact, education of their children, time with their families, access to health care, safer foods, cleaner drinking water, and better access to parks and recreation are not going to be improved by a 10 per cent increase in take-home pay.[2]

Latham had similar views and laid them out in an unconventional speech to the National Press Club in Canberra on 18 February, just after his first bus trip north. 'A good society,' he said, 'requires more than high incomes and government services. It needs strong, healthy relationships within active communities. For too long, government policy has ignored this vital part of our national life. Labor recognises that there is more to life than money. We understand that our community is awash with social problems that will not be solved by government spending alone.'

He posed uncomfortable questions. How was it that the years of globalisation and rapid economic change could deliver prosperity to many Australians, yet leave rafts of them no better or, indeed, worse off? And what about the time pressures of this new world that cause much unhappiness for working families? Some of the Canberra-based commentators were unimpressed and mocked Latham, dismissing his speech as cliché-ridden, intellectual fairyfloss and a ruse to avoid releasing real policy. They had been expecting a speech with hard news.

It was Ross Gittins, the *Sydney Morning Herald*'s influential economics editor and a quirky, qualified accountant, who took the trouble to examine the speech carefully, think about it and write a column that gave many of his readers cause to look closely at Latham. And it was Gittins, some eight months before the election, who foresaw within Latham's words how the election campaign would unfold.

Gittins wrote in the *Herald* on 25 February 2004 that he believed that Latham was on to something. He said Latham had painted a very attractive picture of life under a Labor government less obsessed with economic growth and more conscious of the social problems people faced. It would mine the public's dissatisfaction with constant economic change and their feeling that whoever was gaining from the economy's supposedly fabulous economic performance, it hadn't been them. He mused that perhaps a turning point in politics had been reached and that the election might be fought on the novel issue of whether there was more to life than economics. However, Gittins warned there was a big risk. John Howard would be itching to fight a campaign based upon the economy's performance and to remind people of Keating's 'recession we had to have' and his 17 per cent interest rates. 'No one understands the effectiveness of such an attack better than Labor itself,' Gittins wrote. 'It's what's kept both Kim Beazley and Simon Crean mesmerised in the headlights. Which is why I say that appearing to be anything other than gung-ho for economic growth is high risk for Labor.'

Latham denied he'd filched tactics from Morris's books. Instead he credited Morris with packaging ideas that matched his own and applying better descriptions of how and why they worked. Said Latham: 'I had it worked out and even if Dick Morris says, "well, get out of the firing zone", then what is the agenda that you are going to create that's the alternative? He is not going to give you many clues about that from an American perspective. You have got to do your own, based on Australian issues and policies and that's what I have been doing.'

Dick Morris, however, thought Latham was doing all the right things. In early June he said the Labor leader was on the right track by confronting the real concerns of Australians, not the theoretical concerns of political insiders. Morris wrote in *The Australian*:

> By running on what seem to be soft issues, Latham is not running to the Left or Right of the Liberals, he is running underneath them. The new Labor candidate is articulating proposals that

strike close to voters' hearts and offering the prospect of real results in helping them to deal with real concerns and issues. If Latham is copying anybody's playbook, it is that of Bill Clinton and Tony Blair. He could do worse.

Certainly Latham's borrowing of policies from Clinton and Blair—and the odd speech line—was frequent and quickly became a government weapon. On 20 April 2004, Latham made a speech on Australia's national identity in Sydney in which he said:

> Every 10 year old must be able to log on to the Internet and manage information. Every 14 year old must find the courses and settings which excite their learning interests and give them a hunger for more education. Every 17 year old must be ready to extend their education into post-secondary qualifications.

The passage looked suspiciously like one used by Bill Clinton in his 1997 State of the Union address in which he said:

> Every eight year old must be able to read; every 12 year old must be able to log on to the Internet; every 18 year old must be able to go to college; and every adult American must be able to keep on learning for a lifetime.

The similarities between the two speeches aided the campaign by Peter Costello to nail Latham as a serial plagiarist. Here was a man who'd govern by using the Google search engine on the Internet, Costello said. And Latham did not limit his borrowing of ideas to speeches. He borrowed policies. His Bookstart program, in which parents would get a free book for each child, mirrored the British scheme—also named Bookstart—run by local councils. The United Kingdom had an Aim Higher tertiary education policy. Latham got one too. The United States' Read Aloud program was imported by the

Latham Labor Party. Latham's National Mentoring Foundation for boys had an American parent in Clinton's National Mentoring Partnership. Labor's Bright Futures policy to boost male school teacher numbers was pre-dated by a scheme in the United States.

Parliament was the place for Latham to repair what he knew were potentially serious doubts in the minds of voters, doubts that the government would use every opportunity to cleave open. Howard wanted to sow the notion that Latham was erratic, ill-disciplined and immature. Latham knew that his well-publicised fight with a Sydney taxi driver a few years before offered a foundation for Howard's case. After he was elected leader Latham adopted a remarkable new style. No longer would he snarl across the chamber, rising to the bait of his old foe Tony Abbott. Instead he'd most often sit in his chair, pen in hand and work on correspondence with his head down, seemingly disinterested in taunts from the other side. He went from muscling up to Costello (the term he used when Crean appointed him shadow Treasurer) to a model of parliamentary behaviour. It was a sudden transformation that frustrated the government's frontbench. They wanted an early Latham eruption. Even an angry, unflattering photograph taken of Latham during Question Time would help. Latham gave no opportunity. He was very deliberate about it. 'The government was trying to attack me and say that I was ill-disciplined and erratic. The best way to prove your case is let them be erratic in their attacks on me and just ignore them. So it sort of allowed me to prove my case by using their energy and their attacks on me and just allowing it to go through to the keeper. I had no desire to bite on Abbott and Costello's bait. I was happy enough to let those things wash over me. You are better off sitting there, just quietly, absorbing whatever they have to say and treating it as inconsequential.'[3]

✧

Dick Morris wasn't the only American political strategist to have an influence on Australian federal politics in 2004. John Howard looked to Lee Atwater, the father of wedge politics, for help in his campaign against the elusive Mark Latham. Atwater, who died of cancer at age 40 in 1991, was one of the most loathed and admired men in United States politics for his ability to link his political opponents to support of unpopular social issues. His standout success had been to guide presidential candidate George Bush Snr to victory over Democratic nominee Michael Dukakis in 1988 with a series of incendiary television advertisements that attacked Dukakis— then Governor of Massachusetts—for granting early release to Willie Horton, a black prisoner who later went on a crime rampage. The Horton advertisements have entered political folklore as classic examples of wedge politics.

When the freighter *Tampa* anchored off Christmas Island just before the 2001 election with a load of asylum seekers on board, John Howard had the wedge that ruined Labor leader Kim Beazley's campaign. Throughout the 2004 election year Howard was on the lookout for another wedge issue. Several times he thought he had it—only to be stymied by Latham's refusal to be drawn into the web.

Howard's first attempt to drive in the wedge came with his plan to force Labor's hand on gay marriage. The government's Marriage Legislation Amendment Bill was an attempt to change the country's marriage laws by expressly prohibiting same-sex marriages from having any legal standing. The rationale for the change was said to be to meet popular concern about the sanctity of marriage and also to give formal recognition to the Coalition's ideology that marriage was a voluntary lifelong union between *a male and a female*. But the bill also fitted the definition of a political wedge: its effect was to stigmatise an unpopular group—the gay community—and discredit Labor for supporting them. The trouble was Labor did not oppose the bill. Nicola Roxon, Latham's shadow attorney general, had to go through many contortions to justify her party's position—far from popular within the Left. She eventually explained that 'To fight on the issue of radically changing the definition of marriage, when it is so contested in the community, would risk setting back the cause of same-sex law reform extensively'.[4] Those within Labor who believed that not fighting the bill set back the gay cause bit their tongues. It was about dodging the wedge.

With that failure, Howard used another group to try to wedge Labor—Aborigines. The Aboriginal and Torres Strait Islander Commission (ATSIC), the body established by the Hawke Labor government and charged with representing Aboriginal Australians and delivering services to them, had become pretty much a lame duck. Its chairman, Geoff Clark, had been accused in *The Age* of rape and charged with assault after a pub fight. Latham received information that the Howard government planned to abolish ATSIC and expected the Labor Party, because of its long history of support for Aboriginal causes, to fight the move. Another wedge was landing. Latham long believed that once you saw a wedge issue coming it was better to get out in front of it and deal with it on your terms. He pre-empted Howard and announced a Labor government would abolish ATSIC.

The government saw the intense opposition within the Labor Party and the unions to the Free Trade Agreement (FTA) with the United States as another opportunity to drive in the wedge and damage Latham before the election campaign began. Howard made the signing of the deal by US President George Bush the jewel in the crown of his future economic strategy. He was also happy to allow Australians to credit the government's support of the US in Iraq as buying the agreement. The FTA, according to Howard, offered the promise of a big, lucrative market for Australian exporters of goods and services and fresh waves of American investment in Australia. He portrayed the agreement as being so important for the nation's future that it was somehow above party politics. His appeal to Latham on the issue was to 'call it for Australia, Mr Latham'.

Latham had always been lukewarm on the FTA. He was never convinced that there was an overwhelming case for it, much less that the claimed benefits would be easily recognised by the public. And he knew there was trenchant opposition to the FTA within sections of the arts lobby, the union movement and on the Labor Left. However, he also knew that to oppose the deal might be used to fuel perceptions that he was anti-American, something that would most certainly cost Labor votes in a climate where most Australians placed a high priority on the military alliance with the US. Nothing about the decision would be easy for the Labor Party. It would bleed on the inside if Latham supported the deal, and on the outside if he opposed it. So he decided to play for time. He announced early in 2004 that Labor's final position on the FTA would depend on examination of the details. And that is where Latham stayed for six months until a Senate committee combing through the deal completed its report in early August.

By then the union campaign against the FTA had reached a crescendo, aided by actors concerned about a US cultural invasion under the deal and by the consumer health lobby, who believed the big US drug companies would use their muscle to force up the cost of pharmaceuticals in Australia. Labor's Left became even more strongly fixed against the deal. Howard saw his chance and moved to force Labor to declare its hand by introducing the legislation supporting the FTA into Parliament. Dennis Shanahan, *The Australian*'s political editor, wrote on 3 August 2004, 'Mark Latham's Labor Party has been heading toward today's train wreck for months.' He said Howard's exploitation of Labor's ructions on the FTA were akin to the prime minister's exploitation of the *Tampa* issue. Howard, Shanahan said, had perfectly orchestrated the timing of the FTA debate ahead of the election.

The same day that Shanahan's piece appeared, Latham lobbed one of his fizzing little bombs at a press conference he called that afternoon. Many of the reporters there expected him to announce Labor's support for the FTA. It was thought he would ride out the dissent in his ranks. Instead, Latham said the party would fight like Kilkenny cats to change the FTA's enabling legislation. And, if the government did not agree to two Labor changes, there would be no FTA. It was an unexpected, defiant stand that rocked Howard backwards.

The first change Latham demanded was to protect Australian-made content on free-to-air and subscription radio and television. The second was for stiff penalties to prevent US-domiciled drug companies making spurious legal attempts to extend the life of their patents, thereby stopping cheaper generic drugs from coming on to the Australian market. The fight over the FTA had entered the endgame. Howard miscalculated. He could have simply said that the government would accept the Labor amendments even though they were not needed. There would have been a loss of face, but he would have his FTA. That's pretty well what he did on the first demand. But Howard dug in on the drugs issue. He commissioned legal opinions from five government departments, all of which concluded there was no way to draft a legally enforceable amendment to meet the Opposition's concerns. Then he suggested there was a risk the United States might pull out of the deal if Labor persisted. Then he just gave in, threw up his hands and walked off.

The media counted this as a huge win for Latham. It was said he'd revived after a flat mid-winter. Commentators lauded his tactics. But the truth was much simpler: the amendments weren't even Latham's ideas. He had picked them up after taking home and reading for himself one weekend the lengthy report of the Senate inquiry into the FTA. Latham wanted to recognise the benefits but to be seen as being mindful of the social concerns. He had not designed Labor's position to wrongfoot Howard. Rather, he was deeply worried about the Labor Party hopelessly splitting into pro and anti–FTA factions. Cracks were emerging publicly. What he wanted most was for his own party to hold together.

The *Australian*'s political commentator, Paul Kelly, said:

> There is no doubt that he did wrong-foot John Howard this week. Labor won the week essentially because of Mark Latham's tactics on the FTA and I think it is a warning to the Government on election eve that he is capable of these sort of tactical manoeuvres which can take the Government by surprise.[5]

But the favourable outcome had been far more by luck than design. It was a break Latham needed. Personally, he'd had a rotten few weeks. People drooling over his past and a death had flattened him.

Chapter 7

A Heart in Winter

WORKING IN PARLIAMENT HOUSE IN CANBERRA IS LIKE BEING on board a ship. Inside the long, white walls are bars and restaurants, a coffee shop, post office, travel agency and gym, even a hairdresser, a chapel and a nurse. There are tennis courts as smooth and as green as pool tables. And beneath the building, repair men in overalls with toolkits ride bikes along dim, narrow avenues that crisscross the building's bowels. They keep everything working for the more than 2000 people who sit at desks in the building's carpeted acres above. Pink carpet for the Senate side, light green for the House of Representatives. Most of these workers are sparkly careerists. A lot are single. There is plenty of drinking, casual sex and some drugs.

An outsider might get a view of this other life by visiting one of the bars at Manuka or Kingston on a Wednesday night, before everybody returns to their electorates on Thursday evening. These are the kinds of places that are empty at 9 pm but half an hour later, after Parliament has risen, are loud and busy. In winter, the men wear expensive dark suits and the women long, fine wool overcoats. These are political fixers, minders, journalists and politicians. Many will probably have a partner—but not in Canberra. Most have no need to go home early. Party boundaries are let down on such nights. Sometimes other boundaries fall, too. Some will have a drink and go home alone. Many others will go off in groups to restaurants and carry on into the night. A few might pair off and disappear. It's remarkable on such nights—powered by alcohol, carried by chance and unshackled by distance—that more marriages aren't broken.

The Grange, in the middle of Manuka's restaurant strip, was a hangout for Mark Latham and his drinking buddies, NSW Labor MPs Joel Fitzgibbon and Robert McClelland. It was here, in the middle of 1997, that Mark Latham met Janine Lacey, a tall, blonde, finely featured former Liberal Party staffer from Parliament House who was now working for a Canberra public relations firm. It was at about this time, according to Gabrielle Gwyther's account of the period, that Mark Latham began to stay in Canberra on some weekends. She says he had asked her for an open marriage a few months before while the couple were in Madrid. Gabrielle did not think the question was serious. Instead, she believed Mark was mentally exhausted and under strain, most of it having been brought on by pressure to finish his book *Civilising Global Capital*. She was not overly concerned for the future of her marriage, believing she had no reason to be. After Latham was diagnosed with testicular cancer in 1993—and had a testicle removed—he had been told he would not be a father. Gabrielle felt his illness had brought them closer and she accepted the advice that she would not be a mother. She decided to pour her energy into assisting Latham's Canberra ambitions.

But in December 1997, she left the couple's Sydney home after Mark told her he was seeing Janine Lacey. It was Gabrielle's understanding that she and Mark would try to save their marriage. This was not to be. She found the marriage break-up traumatic and asked that this account appear in this book: 'The relationship between Janine and Mark went on behind my back and I was not in a position to do anything about it. Its revelation was a total shock to me. I was the last to know and their behaviour towards me was disgusting. Mark told his mother and sister, Jody, months before I even had an inkling of the affair. I remain extremely upset at the behaviour of those two human beings toward me, even though I have managed to get on with my life.'[1]

Gabrielle was, however, more explicit to other media about the details of her marriage. On 11 July 2004, the Melbourne *Herald Sun* published Gabrielle's claims that Mark had in 1997 asked for an open marriage. She said her husband had told her he wanted 'new experiences'. Speaking out has diminished Gabrielle's pain: 'I only spoke out because he never ever apologised or acknowledged that I helped him in any way with his career. I know I have taken a lot of flak over this but I feel I have finally got closure on that man.'[2]

The break-up of Latham's marriage to Gabrielle came amid acrimony that has lingered through the years since. Both volunteered intimate and highly damaging claims about each other's pasts for this book.

It was Gabrielle's willingness to talk to journalists about the end of her marriage that contributed much to Latham's mid-winter personal slump. That, and a death, drove him to his bleakest point since becoming Labor leader. It caused him to lose political momentum when he could least afford it. It concerned his staff, who tried to restore his spirits. It revealed a brittleness in his make-up.

When the Tasmanian Labor premier Jim Bacon died aged 54 in late June from lung cancer, Latham realised the older he became, the worse he was affected by death. He felt flat and irritable. He'd got to know Bacon well and had taken a shine to him. In Bacon, Latham saw his own story. The Tasmanian had been a tearaway in his youth, had matured and had gone on to lead the Labor Party. And he'd been the only premier to publicly support Latham for the leadership in the lead-up to the December ballot. Now he was dead. Latham went down to Hobart on a chilly, clear Thursday for the funeral. He tried to conceal his blackness. He dodged the press for a day or two.

In the mid-afternoon a week later an email arrived in Latham's office, sent to his chief of staff, Mike Richards. It was from the *Sydney Morning Herald* and the questions it put to Latham about his past would empty him. Latham already knew the *Herald* was preparing a lengthy article because he had been told that the author of the email, journalist Deborah Snow, had been passing on rumours and stories about his past to her friends and associates. One person who had attended a weekend Sydney dinner party with Snow was concerned enough to email Latham's office. Latham had already refused to be interviewed by Snow, who had previously worked on the ABC's *Four Corners* and had served as the broadcaster's Moscow correspondent. He was now deeply suspicious of the likely content of her story. Deborah Snow strongly denies that she or her *Herald* colleague, Damien Murphy, deliberately passed on stories and rumours about Latham's past and responded to Latham's allegations by saying: 'In preparing our report we adhered to the normal processes experienced and ethical journalists employ to research and test the lines of inquiry generated by a major profile of this sort.'[3]

The email from Deborah Snow and Damien Murphy is reproduced below with Latham's reply because it is pivotal to the onset of his bleakness and his decision to confront the rumours in an extraordinary public fashion.

From: Deborah Snow
Sent: Thursday, 1 July 2004 2:46 pm
To: Mike Richards

Subject: Questions for Mr Latham as discussed, from Deborah Snow and Damien Murphy.

1) We understand you sought pre-selection for the seat of Fowler in 1984. If so, was it with any real expectation of winning, or just an exercise to test the process?

2) Which dates and in which positions did you work in John Kerin's and Bob Carr's offices? We note that the Whitlam Institute website refers to you working for Bob Carr continuously through 1988–91. However you left Carr after the Liverpool by-election, before later returning. Can your office supply correct dates please?

3) It has been claimed that with the best of intentions you and Joel Fitzgibbon had Greg Wilton [the Labor MP] discharged from hospital shortly before his suicide? Is this so? If not, have you any comments to make about this tragic episode?

4) On a lighter note, colleagues recall you once charging the bar bill for a Labor officials meeting to John Faulkner as a joke? Is this correct? [Faulkner does not drink.]

5) Your former wife, Gabrielle, makes several claims about the final stages of your marriage:
  –that you asked for an open marriage during a trip to Spain with her in 1997
  –that you detailed to her several affairs you were having
  –that you flew to join your present wife, Janine, in Perth in November 1997 for a holiday before you and Gabrielle had fully separated
  –that you continued to see Gabrielle through much of the course of 1998 and sustained a relationship with her while you embarked on your relationship with your present wife
Do you dispute or have any other comment to make on these claims?

6) Gabrielle also talks of you asking the proprietor at a restaurant during her 30th birthday dinner to put on a video called 'Freaks of Nature' which she says was pornographic and embarrassed guests. A member of her family confirms this account.

Gabrielle maintains that you have 'dined out' frequently on this episode. Do you have any comment on it?

7) Have you any comment on the perception among parliamentary colleagues during 1997–98 that a group with which you were linked socially was actively seeking to 'bed' Liberal staffers? Do you have any knowledge of such activities?

8) What is your comment, if any, on the chain of events which led to Gary Gray raising concerns with Gough Whitlam about your approaches to a Liberal staffer? Was that person working in the office of Warwick Parer?

9) What is your relationship with Carl Habib? Have you any comment on the events at your buck's night staged at his panel beating workshop?

10) Have you any comment on a neighbour's and Gabrielle's claim that one of your sisters was under the care of the Department of Youth and Community Services for a period in the aftermath of your father's death?

We remain willing to discuss any of these matters with you or your office off the record if you do not wish to respond formally. Thank you.

From: Mike Richards
Sent: Monday, 5 July 9.22 AM
To: Deborah Snow

Subject: Re questions for Mr Latham as discussed, from Deborah Snow and Damien Murphy.

Dear Deborah/Damien. Mark has considered your email and I append his responses to your questions below.

Best regards
Mike

2 July 2004

Response to Deborah Snow and Damien Murphy

In recent weeks, several friends and associates of Deborah Snow have conveyed to me the disgusting rumours that she has been spreading about me and my family (including at a dinner party in Sydney several weekends ago and on other occasions).

Even if she now writes nothing, her unprofessional actions have started a rumour mill that, unhappily, my family and I will have to live with for some time to come. This is not journalism. It is titillation and rumour-mongering.

As for the questions that have been submitted, this is my response.

1) Bit of both.

2) I am not responsible for the content of the Whitlam Institute website nor for passing on any contacts.

3) That is not true. How would Joel Fitzgibbon or I have had the authority to discharge Greg from hospital?

4) Yes.

5) Gabrielle Gwyther has given many media interviews making false claims against me and my family. I dealt with the break-up of my first marriage seven months ago when Gabrielle Gwyther first raised it in the media. I have dealt with it since in numerous interviews with newspapers and book authors. Not surprisingly, Gabrielle Gwyther and I have different points of view as to how and why our marriage ended. I really don't see the need to make any further comment.

6) I had never heard of the video 'Freaks of Nature' until the owner of the restaurant himself decided to put it on towards the end of the evening. (He owned a video shop next door.)

7–8) As friends do, Gough Whitlam informed me of a rumour that was circulating and I informed him it was untrue. Unfortunately, there are many rumours and 'perceptions' in politics, opposed to facts. The rumours you have raised in these two questions are untrue.

9) Carl Habib is a businessman and prominent citizen in my electorate. My buck's night 13 years ago was not held at his panelbeating workshop.

10) My father died in 1981. I did not meet Gabrielle Gwyther until 1987. As with other claims she has made against my family for the period proceeding [sic] 1987, she would not know. In any case, my sisters are not public figures and to the best of my knowledge, this claim is false.

MARK LATHAM

At least one of the questions—number 8—was based on a fallacy. None of the women who worked at Senator Warwick Parer's office can recall any unwanted attention from Latham. However, there was a Labor senator whose frequent visits became unwelcome.

The *Sydney Morning Herald* wasn't alone in its extensive digging into Latham's past. Channel Nine's *Sunday* program had been at work for weeks on a profile of Latham that would go to air on Sunday 4 July 2004, two days after Latham fired off his curt reply to the *Herald*'s questions. Latham had also refused to talk to *Sunday*'s reporter Ross Coulthart, a sharp, lanky New Zealander who'd qualified as a lawyer, crossed the Tasman and made a name for himself as a serious investigative journalist. Latham had surprised Coulthart and the program's executive producer, former *Herald* editor John Lyons, by refusing to be interviewed. Latham contended he no longer had time to cooperate because it would mean several lengthy interviews and require him to make his home available to a camera crew. Besides, *Sunday* had already profiled him in mid 2002—well before he became leader—and he'd cooperated then.

Privately, Latham had other reasons for refusing to speak to *Sunday*. He'd become aware that the program was looking closely at some of his early Labor Party battles in Sydney's south-west and was also combing through his period as mayor of Liverpool. Latham believed the program was out to do a job on him. He knew Lyons and Coulthart had both made their reputations for their investigative work, and believed that was the way the program would approach any profile of him as leader. In Latham's mind, *Sunday* wanted to produce *the* piece of investigative journalism that brought about his downfall. The program would be looking for his scalp. He decided he would not assist them and instead would deal with whatever they turned up after the program went to air.

Lyons believed that a current affairs program of the calibre of *Sunday* could not afford to go through the election year without having produced a program on the new leader of the Labor Party. He insisted it be made even without Latham. Naturally, Latham's refusal to appear didn't make for a positive program. In the days before it went to air, word went out that it contained explosive revelations. Newspaper columnists, doubtless encouraged by Channel Nine's publicity machine, hyped up its content. Expectations of damaging revelations were high.

Two days before *Sunday* went to air, Latham gave an interview to Sydney radio broadcaster John Laws. He made this decision after Coulthart revealed that *Sunday* would give a fresh airing to an allegedly violent incident Latham had been involved in fifteen years before. Latham's move was intended to prick *Sunday*'s bubble. As Latham told Laws, claims by Labor Party member Don Nelson that he had been punched by the Labor leader had already been reported in *The Age* on 13 March 2004. The revelation had caused no reaction.

A less apparent reason for Latham's decision to do the Laws interview was the *Sydney Morning Herald*'s questions, which pointed to the likely content of the *Herald*'s upcoming article.

Latham tried to head off revelations that might suggest more than a few sexual liaisons by giving Laws the quote that was most used in the next day's newspaper reports of the interview. He told Laws: 'Can I just give you the breaking news—I had an active love life before marriage. Now imagine what the Liberal Party will do with that. I can hardly wait for Tony Abbott's diatribe to the Australian Parliament—ooh, what a person!'

When it was screened, the *Sunday* program added to the mosaic of Latham's life; it didn't change the image. It steered away from his past private life. Bob Hawke admitted he'd misjudged Latham (Hawke had supported Beazley for the leadership); Liverpool Council's former general manager, a Liberal supporter, was lavish in his praise for Latham; and old Don Nelson threw punches at the air on camera, reliving his long-ago stoush with a future Labor leader. The Nelson interview, despite recounting events that had happened fifteen years before, was damaging to Latham because it confirmed in some minds that he was a volatile person. The story that Latham had more recently crash-tackled a Sydney taxi driver after a fare dispute was already well known.

When Latham's office told the press gallery the next day—Monday—that the Labor leader was going to hold an unscheduled, full press conference in Parliament House at about 11 am, the gallery was caught by surprise. None of the *Sunday* program's content was explosive. There seemed no obvious running issue. When Latham strode up to the podium in front of curious journalists his purpose was immediately clear: 'Thanks very much for coming. I've called this press conference to clear the air. Sometime in the next couple of months we are going to have an election campaign and I believe it should be about the positive things we should be doing for Australia's future rather than the old politics of fear and smear.'

What unfolded was one of the strangest press conferences ever held at Parliament House. Latham outed himself, saying he'd been the subject of an onslaught of rumours and smears. He laid them out one by one before an incredulous press gallery and rejected each one. It was as if he was scurrying to pick up fizzing bombs and hurl them back at his enemies. Surely, one would go off and blow off his hands. He resurrected old and painful secrets that most of the journalists had never before heard, such as the accusation laid at him in 1998 that he'd sexually harassed a parliamentary staffer. He denied it. That there was a video of him in a compromising situation at the buck's night before his first marriage. Not so.

The toughest words to get out came four minutes after he began. 'It seems to me that these rumours come from three sources—it's no surprise that one is the first wife. She was out in the media in December and she's been backgrounding journalists ever since. Well, my standard is simply this: I refuse to relive a marriage break-up publicly. It was hard enough the first time. I am not going through it a second time in the public arena and I don't believe the Australian people see it as my public duty to do that. She has remarried with children and so have I. At the time it was hard. It was messy. I would've made mistakes. I mean, there were things that you just wouldn't believe. It's the toughest part of your life. If anyone has had a perfect marriage break-up, let me know about it—I don't think anyone ever has. The only request I make—and it's a request I made in December, it might not have been noted at the time—as these rumours are circulated from my first wife, and some people in the media repeat them, would you lay off my family? Things have been said to me about my sisters, my mother, my father that are not true and they don't deserve it. Say whatever you like about me but leave them out of it. Please.'

Painful memories and the protectiveness felt for his mother and sisters welled up inside him and almost choked him. He didn't cry, but he almost did.

Latham then identified two other sources of the rumours.

One was a group of former Liverpool councillors, including Casey Conway and Frank Heyhoe, who he said remained disgruntled over his rise to the Liverpool mayoralty. He also claimed that a special government unit, based in Parliament House, existed for the purpose of gathering unfavourable material about him and the Labor Party. Latham stood at the podium for 35 minutes and answered 38 questions until journalists had no more. One woman journalist from the Murdoch press had repeatedly shrieked at the Labor leader: 'Do you believe in fidelity?' Throughout, Latham was by turns stoic, defiant, testy, vulnerable.

The media conference had been called at short notice, so some of the press gallery's regular political correspondents didn't make it. Lauren Martin, a savvy mid-western American who usually writes about art for the *Sydney Morning Herald*, did. She happened to be in the *Herald*'s Parliament House office and took the chance to see a Latham press conference. Knowing the paper would want the story from its specialist political writers, she scurried off without a pen. That afternoon, she was asked to write about the press conference. Her piece in the next day's paper stood out as a vivid assessment of Latham's performance. Martin wrote: 'If the aim of the whispering campaigns was to provoke the inner brute in the Opposition Leader, it backfired yesterday. Latham took on each nasty, unsubstantiated rumour—sexual harassment, strippers at his buck's night, violence, infidelity—and addressed them with tenderness.'

Many, however, were critical of Latham's decision to confront the rumours publicly. Bob Carr knew that John Faulkner had remonstrated with a distraught Latham on the weekend before the press conference. Carr later made a revealing entry in his diary about the episode.

Latham had been crying throughout Saturday and faced a screaming match with Faulkner who tried to insist that Latham not mention his first wife. But he couldn't help himself. Discipline said [Carr's source named here] in the end, discipline. Only one subject of interest—Latham's apparent crack-up. Calling a press conference to denounce rumours, sexual harassment, a bucks night video, sister. It was mad. Nobody was going to print this low rent stuff but he cracked. Appalling press conference. Fighting back crocodile tears. Mike Rann [the South Australian premier] said to me 'he lost the men when he cried, he lost the women when he blamed his ex-wife. You never attack a woman.' I told Kevin Rudd to stay away as long as he can [Rudd was in China].

Though few people knew it at the time, the *Sydney Morning Herald* had been very much in Latham's mind that morning when he told his staff he had decided to call a full press conference to deal with the rumours about his past. The previous Saturday morning Louise Dodson, the newspaper's Canberra political correspondent, said in a front-page article that Latham had yet to respond to 'reports of a raunchy video taken at his buck's night before his first marriage'. Dodson had no confirmation that such a video existed, but her report was immediately picked up by another of the press gallery's heavy hitters, Murdoch columnist Glen Milne, who wrote about the video in his syndicated Sunday newspaper column the next day. At least Milne had the good grace to later admit he'd lifted the video claim from Dodson's unsubstantiated *Herald* story.

Latham knew the gallery was tearing at his flesh. He had to stop it. He felt overwhelmed. Aside from the video rumour, he knew the *Sydney Morning Herald*'s feature article was likely to be salacious and that *Sunday* had given new life to mostly true stories that had already been published about the political bloodletting that had occurred during his rise through the Labor Party in Sydney's south-west. He could see the stories going for another week or two—unless he picked himself up and confronted the lot.

Latham's view that some in the media had entered a reckless phase concerning his past was confirmed within a few hours of his press conference. Sydney radio broadcaster Steve Price put to air a call from a man who claimed to have seen the rumoured buck's night video. The next morning Price demonstrated true idiocy when he appeared on Channel Seven's *Today Show* and said there was no doubt the video existed. He was certain, he said, because the man who'd phoned him had given his contact details. Latham, by then, was in Brisbane and he was drained and furious. He told his staff he wanted an apology and a retraction from Price. That night Price was back on air and now said his informant had admitted the video story was an invention. 'Now, I am not sure where that leaves us,' Price told his listeners lamely.

About a week before the arrival of Snow's questions, Mike Richards had been on a quiet mission to see the editor of the *Sydney Morning Herald*, Robert Whitehead. Richards had once been a deputy editor of *The Age*, a Fairfax-owned title like the *Sydney Morning Herald*. He and Whitehead had served together on the Fairfax executive management team and knew each other reasonably well. They went for coffee and Richards raised Latham's deep concerns about Deborah Snow. Richards did not want her removed from the Latham story, nor did he seek to influence the content of the article, but he did want Snow warned not to spread stories about Latham's past.

The arrival of Snow's email confirmed in Latham's mind the likely character of the article the *Sydney Morning Herald*, arguably the nation's most influential newspaper, was preparing. Such questions would alarm any public figure. Latham was upset and angry. The day after his Canberra press conference, he pointed the finger at the *Herald* in an interview on Brisbane radio, saying he was disgusted by Snow's question about his sister, which she said related to something that never happened.

And he rounded on Snow's colleague Damien Murphy for contacting the woman who'd been his second wife's dancing teacher when she was fifteen years old. He said such questions had led to his emotional appeal the day before for journalists to leave his family alone.

The *Herald*'s editors had not decided at the outset to concentrate on Latham's private past. Rather, the newspaper was a victim of its own tardiness in not publishing a definitive, in-depth story on Latham when he became leader. Its Murdoch-owned rival, *The Australian*, had produced a lengthy article in its weekend magazine about Latham's relationship with his father. Kerry Packer's *Bulletin* magazine had published a long story on Latham's rise on the very day Simon Crean was told his leadership was over. Even its sister paper, *The Age*, had scooped the *Herald* on its own turf by running a revealing account of Latham's period as a Sydney local politician. The *Herald*'s problem was how to catch up.

Snow and Murphy, two very different journalists, were chosen to research and write the story. Murphy is a broad bear of a man in his 50s. He is a regular surfer with a deeply laconic air and a man most at ease with ordinary people living ordinary lives. Snow is an intense, serious woman whose journalistic interests tend towards politics and policy detail. Naturally, it was Murphy who went to Sydney's far western suburbs and knocked on doors looking for Latham's past. He'd already decided that much of the Latham story already published was largely uncritical. The silences and evasions he encountered to his questions about Latham's relationships with women gave him an idea for the angle the story should take. He found Gabrielle Gwyther. Although she had allowed other journalists to visit her home and discuss her former husband, the details she gave Murphy on the record stand as an explicit portrait of Latham's doomed first marriage

The newspaper published a two-part series which began on Saturday 11 July. Spread across three pages, the first instalment was headlined 'MARK LATHAM—A LEADER IN PROFILE'. In truth it was vastly narrower, but nevertheless a big and juicy read. It concentrated on Latham's sexual past. It aired rumours that he had been associated with a group of Labor MPs and staffers who competed to seduce Liberal staffers. It was the kind of article the *Herald*'s readers on Sydney's north shore and in the eastern suburbs would savour right to the end, and then profess to being appalled by the journalism. Indeed, it was difficult to move through the *Herald*'s Sydney territories that weekend and not have conversation about the newspaper's article on Latham. It did enormous damage.

It is true that Latham had once earned a reputation in Canberra. He cracked on to women. On some accounts, he could be blunt. It is also true that an interest in a parliamentary staffer had come to the attention of Kim Beazley when he was leader because some of Latham's colleagues had been concerned by what they viewed as his erratic behaviour. After Labor senator Nick Sherry attempted suicide in Canberra, an informal compact was put in place between the offices of the leader of the Opposition and the prime minister that if there were concerns about the state of mind of a parliamentarian, it would be reported to the party leader before the other side made use of it. It was under this agreement that Beazley was informed of Latham's behaviour. Latham denied any wrong doing. He was infuriated that the incident was included in the *Herald*'s article. The entire article badly wounded him. He was angry with the *Herald* and Snow, and he privately raged against Gwyther. He could not understand why she persisted in denigrating him when she had remarried, had a child and had, ostensibly, got on with her life.

After Gabrielle and Mark parted for good, Mark's mother and sisters bought her a gold bracelet. It took away little of her pain and fear: 'I knew that until I could speak out in public about what I thought about him, that I was always going to be scared of him. And I don't feel scared of him any more.'[3]

The questions over Latham's private life died away. By August his spirit had recovered. But, once again, his past would tear him down. An old illness had left its scar.

Chapter 8

The Court of the King

AT DUSK ON A TUESDAY IN MID-AUGUST BOB HAWKE CALLED into Mark Latham's downtown Sydney office in the Phillip Street legal district. Just back from a trip to Asia, Hawke wanted to talk election tactics. It had been a long afternoon for Latham. He'd had various MPs through his office, a meeting with the rock singer Peter Garrett who'd been shoe-horned into the old Sydney Labor seat of Kingsford Smith, and now Hawke. Still, Latham was feeling and looking far better than he'd been a month before when he'd been overwhelmed by rumours and scuttlebutt about his past. His bleakness had lifted and his colour had returned.

The pair sank into the pale lemon couches in Latham's office. Their relationship had warmed since Hawke's public concession in early July that he had been wrong to have favoured Kim Beazley over Latham for the leadership. Minutes into the meeting, Latham began to feel a tummy rumble. It quickly turned into an intense pain in the stomach. Fearing he was suffering from food poisoning, Latham interrupted Hawke: 'Look, Bob, I'm crook. We'll have to end the meeting.' Hawke went out and told Latham's staff, 'This boy needs a doctor.' Glenn Byres, Latham's press secretary, rushed in and saw Latham writhing on the couch. He went for a phone to call a doctor but because it was close to 6 pm, Byres realised most nearby surgeries would be closing. The only doctor he knew who might be in running distance was the NSW deputy premier, Dr Andrew Refshauge. Refshauge had worked with the Aboriginal Medical Service before entering the NSW Parliament. The tall, gentle figure from Labor's Left was in his ministerial office in the Governor Macquarie Tower planning his schedule for the next day. He hurried out of the building and sprang the short distance to Latham's office. Byres met him in the foyer and they caught the lift up.

Refshauge found Latham slumped on the couch. His face was contorted with pain. It was obviously far more serious than food poisoning. The possibilities flashed through Refshauge's mind: a serious bowel obstruction, appendicitis or a major infection. Then, when Latham said he was getting stabbing pains in the shoulder, Refshauge narrowed the likely cause. He knew that irritation or pressure on the stomach diaphragm bounced pain through nerves in the shoulder area. He suspected pancreatitis—a severe inflammation of the pancreas.

At its worst pancreatitis can cause a myriad of complications and be life threatening. Severe cases may bring on dehydration and low blood pressure. The heart, lungs or kidneys might fail. If bleeding occurs in the pancreas, shock and sometimes even death follow. Refshauge asked Latham's staff to ring around the emergency departments of central Sydney hospitals. He wanted Latham admitted immediately, although the stricken Labor leader had narrowed the options by insisting that he would only go to a public hospital. Sydney Hospital in nearby Macquarie Street could take him immediately. Refshauge called the hospital's medical registrar to brief him on Latham's condition. He wanted to avoid a situation where the Labor leader was whisked into an operating theatre and put under the knife without proper consideration of his condition. With Latham slumped in the front seat, his driver raced through the city peak hour traffic to hospital, a few buildings down from the NSW Parliament. Latham's chief of staff, Mike Richards, was in the backseat and guided the shuffling Labor leader into the arms of waiting medical staff.

Refshauge's suspicion was right. Tests confirmed pancreatitis and Latham was transferred to nearby St Vincents Hospital. He soon recovered but the cause remained a mystery. He was not a frequent heavy drinker, nor did he have gallstones—the two common causes of the condition. Latham's best theory for his illness, based on what he'd been told by his doctors, was that the radiotherapy treatment for testicular cancer he'd undergone a decade before might have damaged his pancreas. The upshot was a dry election campaign for Latham and simple foods. He was ordered off alcohol for at least three months. He gave up chilli-laced dishes and curries.

The attack caused Latham's staff to wonder whether a similar incident in his Canberra office three months before was not the food poisoning Latham believed it to be. Then, he had been due to deliver an evening speech in Canberra, away from Parliament. In the late afternoon he complained of stomach pain. He threw up. He said he felt crook but believed he'd be able to give his speech. He promptly threw up again. His deputy, Jenny Macklin, delivered his speech that night.

The Sydney attack of pancreatitis was a window into the workings of the Latham court. Hawke was with him when he became ill and a Labor Party doctor was the first to be called. Mike Richards, the man who jumped into the car as Latham was being ferried to hospital, was steeped in Victorian Labor politics. And the person who appeared on television with updates on Latham's condition was Senate leader John Faulkner from the party's Left, who was one of Latham's closest parliamentary colleagues. Latham had surrounded himself with Labor insiders. They were the people he trusted, with whom he felt comfortable. He took little advice from outside the group. In fact, as some of them later learned, he took little advice anyway.

By late May, six months into his leadership, Latham had spent an average of only one night in three at home. The demands of office meant that Janine and his little boys had been replaced with five fairly constant travelling companions drawn from his Canberra staff of nineteen. They could be seen on TV fleetingly, hovering in the background, avoiding the cameras, and carrying briefing notes and bags while their master drank tea in a church hall or a milkshake on a street walk.

It was something of a breakthrough that they were there at all. When he ascended to the Labor leadership, Latham could not understand why a staff member had to go everywhere with him. He resisted it. His staff persuaded him that, at the very least, he wouldn't be able to carry all the briefing notes and press releases that accompany a leader—not to mention the stuff he'd be given. However, he refused to give up his beige Magna, which he'd drive down the Hume Highway from his Sydney home to Canberra. More often than not he spurned the car and driver that was available to the leader of the Opposition and drove himself between Parliament House and his small flat in Queanbeyan. Soon after becoming leader, he surprised staff at Government House in Canberra when he pulled up alone in the Magna, stopping at the front door to make an official call on the governor general. At the outset his staff were enthused, driven and fiercely loyal to this new look leader.

Mike Richards, Latham's chief of staff, had signalled his arrival in Canberra around the middle of 2003 when most of the Labor Party's staff in the national Parliament squeezed into a room to hear him make a speech that rebuked them. When it was over, they clapped. Brought in by Crean to report on what was wrong with his office set up, Richards was a good looking man in his late 50s with a mane of lush grey hair. Something of a polymath, he holds a PhD in political science and has worked as an academic, a journalist, management consultant, company executive, political advisor and speech writer. He'd spent half a life researching and writing a widely acclaimed book about Ronald Ryan, the last man to hang in Australia. As a management consultant equipped with a University of Melbourne education, he had access into the upper rungs of the Melbourne business community and had been former Victorian premier John Cain's closest advisor. Later, he joined another Victorian institution as deputy CEO of the company that published *The Age*.

Richards had a track record as a fixer of dysfunctional political offices. Only months into his prime ministership, Paul Keating called on Richards to review the workings of his staff. Richards found Keating's office overloaded with economists. Their desktop Reuters screens flashed instant information from the world's financial markets; the work-a-day world of most ordinary Australians was as remote to them as Mars. Richards made few friends among the Keating staff when he quickly concluded many were incapable of getting their heads around what he calls the flim flam and vaudeville—the headline food and political bomb-making that every prime minister's office had to be capable of.

When Richards rebuked staff at that mid year meeting, he also told them they had to stop being risk averse. Risks had to be taken in politics because without risks there was no prospect of political advance. He was urging a far bolder Opposition. It was disgraceful, he said, that in the 2001 election nobody knew what Labor stood for. In taking the job with Crean, Richards believed that Labor needed to go into Parliament and roll grenades. He didn't know it then but Crean would soon be gone and a natural grenade roller would replace him.

Richards had his bags and boxes packed and labelled ready to be shipped out of the Opposition leader's office when

Michael Cooney, a youngish international relations expert and Latham's loyal chief advisor, walked into his office. Latham, the new leader, was about to offer Richards the job of chief of staff. You'd better have an answer, Cooney told him. Richards had doubts. He knew Latham to be a very different personality from his own. If the job went badly, he'd be spending his time cleaning up Latham's shit.

Richards agreed to take the job, but soon developed private doubts about his decision. It became apparent, especially to those staff who came over from Simon Crean, that Latham did not altogether welcome unsolicited advice. There were occasions when he would respond with the tetchy question, 'Did I ask for that?' He would cut staff off in meetings. Just write it up, he'd tell them. Richards, however, did put his stamp upon Latham's office. He made sure that the party's polling was shown to everybody so they knew whether they were succeeding or not. He promised the privilege would be withdrawn if the results ever leaked. They weren't. He moved Latham's media unit in with the policy advisors, believing both groups would benefit from working closer together. And he ran the office day-to-day following established processes. Latham, on the other hand, was impatient. He always wanted to run hard and fast.

As most of Latham's senior staff came over from Crean's office, it was inevitable that tensions would arise. Latham installed one of the bigger personalities into the difficult job of pulling together the major policies for the election year cauldron. Michael Cooney, who had virtually been Latham's sole Canberra staffer for the eighteen months after he returned from the backbench, was a practising Catholic, former army reserve officer, anti-abortionist and, at 33 years of age a father of five. At first blush, he seemed an unlikely figure to find a rapport with someone who had travelled as far outside of the establishment as the agnostic Latham had. But he did share Latham's wriggling mass of contradictions and it was this that most drew them together after Cooney's wife began working for Latham in Canberra in the late 1990s.

Cooney had followed Latham's career and was drawn by what he thought were his progressive ideas and his irreverence. He also liked Latham's direct manner. Latham, he realised, didn't normally hold back on what he thought. Cooney found this refreshing in an era when many politicians were prone to explain at length what they did not think. He also noted that Latham did not bring a single ideology to solving the problems that occupied him. He was willing to be much more pragmatic than most politicians and switch ideologies and theories to meet different challenges. Cooney and Latham had very similar views on economic management and finding fairer ways to deliver education and health services. They also shared a larrikin streak. In a moment long celebrated in Latham's office, Cooney gate-crashed John Howard's media Christmas party at the Lodge one year and introduced himself to Howard before the prime minister's amused staff gently suggested he finish his drink and leave.

Tensions inevitably arose between Cooney and Richards. This can probably be explained by Latham's initial decision to appoint Richards over Cooney to the most senior job in the office but it was exacerbated later in the year when it became clear that Latham had moved Richards to the outer circle while Cooney remained on the inner. The gradual side-lining of Mike Richards by Latham weakened the functioning of the leader's office. It probably contributed to mistakes including Latham's poor relationship with top business leaders, and the debacle of the election campaign's final week in Tasmania.

The Richards appointment was an early mistake by Latham. Their differences were so vast—as Richards himself recognised—that there was a strong possibility of their relationship breaking down. Richards had long experience running big political offices. Latham had worked as a junior in only one— Bob Carr's when he was NSW Opposition leader. Richards cared for order and proper process. Latham was impatient and impetuous.

Latham may well have expected Richards to offer him more political advice and, it appears, less advice on how to run an orderly office. Latham said after the election that he was surprised that Richards had not offered more advice. 'Richards was an office manager, not a political advisor,' Latham said.[1] To many in the office, it was no surprise once it became clear that Latham's relationship with Richards was fracturing that Cooney would be confirmed within the inner circle, along with Byres and Latham's deputy chief of staff, Simon Banks. Banks was a softly spoken lawyer with years of experience advising senior Labor figures and was highly regarded for his tactical judgement. He had a gentle personality that did not lean toward confrontation with Latham.

Cooney remained within Latham's diminished inner circle to the end. So too did Glenn Byres, a tall, tousle-haired blond who fronted up to the Opposition leader's office in late January wearing a dark suit and tie in the faintly unfamiliar manner a farmer wears a suit to a wedding. In his early 30s, Byres liked a drink and a smoke and was an avid sports fan. (His father was the well-known international rugby referee, Dick Byres.) Byres came from the NSW mid-north coast and had never worked in Canberra. But his youth and laconic manner belied a decade of experience working at senior levels for the Carr government in NSW and, later, with the Sydney political lobbying firm Hawker Britton. He had a reputation for being sharp and staying calm. He'd developed a sensitive political radar and an ability to get along with people from many different levels and backgrounds. And he'd come strongly recommended by Latham's old workmates in Bob Carr's office, Bruce Hawker and David Britton, the principals of Hawker Britton. Latham took Byres on and as the election year progressed, Byres travelled at Latham's side almost everywhere. He didn't shy from offering advice to Latham but adopted a laidback tone and didn't repeat himself. Byres relationship with Latham was the best among the travelling staffers.

There was only one woman in a senior position in Latham's office. Vivian Schenker had worked on the ABC's Radio National and on SBS television. She was an experienced, well-regarded journalist who'd worked as a media advisor to Simon Crean. Latham kept her on as his director of communications. A major part of her job was to get Latham into or onto the most appropriate media outlet for the particular message he was trying to communicate. She also chose locations for press conferences and other media events. Schenker, who shared Mike Richards' liberal leanings on social policy, tempered with his dryer views on economics, warmed to Latham. She liked his bad-boy past, the crazy-brave in him, his edginess. Some women told her they found Latham sexy because of those things. Schenker tried to tinker with Latham's image. She thought his glasses cut across his face at exactly the wrong place and obscured his eyes. But Latham would have none of it. Janine had told him his glasses looked good and were fashionable.

It was Schenker who tried valiantly to lift Latham's spirits after Nine's *Sunday* program and the *Sydney Morning Herald* began delving into his past. The depth of his mood slump surprised her. He was dubbed by some in the press gallery Mogadon Man—a reference to the commonly used drug treatment to assist sleeping.

When the *Sydney Morning Herald*'s Louise Dodson wrote a column that began 'Where is Mark Latham?', it was Schenker who urged Latham to lift himself up rather than avoid reporters, to simply tell journalists who pressed him on his past that he'd already dealt with it. But Latham retreated further into the company of the three people in his office to whom he was closest—Cooney, Byres and Simon Banks.

Schenker was not prepared for the blokey culture within the Labor Party. She'd never before worked in an organisation that put so few women into senior positions. And she believed it was this culture—as it extended into Latham's office—that began the undoing of her relationship with the Labor leader. But she was not the only one to have a less than ideal working relationship with the Labor leader.

Latham's speech writer was the Melbourne historian and author Dennis Glover. Glover was a deep thinker and a fine writer. He'd worked for the former Victorian Labor leader John Brumby and then spent five years at Cambridge University where he'd finished a PhD in history. He'd returned to Australia and worked for Beazley as speech writer and then for his successor, Crean. In his years in Britain, Glover became a student of Tony Blair's New Labour. While working for Crean he struck up a rapport with Latham, who shared Glover's belief that Blair's Third Way offered ideas for the ALP. Glover maintained a loyal silence when some of his drafts came back bearing the word 'crap' in Latham's handwriting. It didn't anger him. Glover considered it the absolute right of the leader to reject speech notes, especially one such as Latham who believed that leaders should as much as possible produce speeches that were authentic. But he did think it childish. It was undeserved.

There were those within the office who believed that Latham's speeches suffered because they lacked an elegance and empathy that Glover could have brought to them or the charm of a Bill Clinton or Tony Blair speech, who would most often seek to persuade. Latham's speeches were blunter, but there was also something genuine about them because of his desire to explain policy by using colloquial language and tales from his life story. Like Paul Keating, Latham was often flat when delivering a written speech. As the community forums showed, he was at his best without notes and when the audience feedback animated him.

It was Alex Sanchez who should have been the closest in the office to Latham. They had known each other for over twenty years, mainly through their involvement in the Labor

Party and Liverpool Council where Sanchez had been deputy mayor. Sanchez, a practising Catholic in his early 40s who held a masters degree in economics, was hired by Latham as an economic policy advisor when he was shadow Treasurer. Sanchez took the job because he believed it a once in a lifetime chance to help craft national economic policy. He became disillusioned with his friend and the job when Latham became Opposition leader, but stayed on until Latham resigned. They later rekindled their relationship.

More than anybody else, Sanchez stood up to Latham because he'd spent years working alongside him—not for him. And he believed Latham had too many 'Yes' men working for him. But he eventually came to think of himself not as the advisor he was hired to be but as a 'writer-upper'. The term reflected Latham's frequent instruction to Sanchez to 'go and write it up'. When he attempted to offer advice, he was brushed off. Sanchez thought Latham had become tense and distracted in the leader's job, and that his old friend's sense of humour was being pushed well into the background. But it was to Sanchez that Latham turned when Gabrielle Gwyther first spoke to journalists about the trials of her marriage and separation.

On the Monday morning after the first article appeared, Latham asked Sanchez why he thought Gabrielle had spoken so unflatteringly about their life together. Sanchez said he didn't know but expressed concern about the effect these stories would have on both their children in years to come. Latham looked down at the floor and said he understood. It was a rare moment of candour between the two.

Sanchez believed that in Canberra, away from Janine and the boys, Latham became a loner and a lonely man. He was also distracted by others. He came to think of his old friend as being like a harried Formula One racing driver—travelling at breakneck speed but too often looking in his mirror to see what was coming from behind.

✧

For the former Crean staff, Latham's long thought-out positions and his willingness to take a stand were a big and welcome change. Crean often had to be prodded hard for his views by staff charged with writing his speeches and press releases. And he would weigh himself down with advice and then end up agonising before taking a position.

But it appeared to many of the ex-Crean staff who stayed with the new leader that Latham lacked an understanding of how an orderly political office should work. They thought he operated like a magpie. He'd peck at the ideas he liked and implement them himself. He saw his office as an extension of his own arms and legs. He directed, he ordered. There wasn't much consultation. There were no proper staff meetings. It was a far cry from the inclusive style practised in the political office most people know best—TV's *West Wing*. Some of Crean's former staffers felt they had at least been working towards a higher purpose. With Latham, they detected that the purpose was Latham. And they had been used to working for a politician comfortable with lots of staff. There had been 23 in Crean's office. Latham had never before had a staff of more than three or four.

Latham was therefore very receptive when John Faulkner told him Crean's system of having a raft of policy advisors working out of the leader's office should be dumped. Faulkner urged Latham to restore the policy power balance by pushing many of those policy advisors out of the leader's office and into the offices of his shadow ministers. This gelled very easily with his aim of making shadow ministers much more responsible for determining the central issues of their portfolios and crafting policies around them. Latham, of course, had bitter experience of what it was like for a shadow minister to have policy forced upon him when Beazley's office gutted his education policy in the 1998 election and told him of the changes only hours before the policy was announced. Latham was also well aware of what he referred to as the awkwardness for senior shadow ministers when they had to answer to a policy advisor in the party leader's office. He wanted his shadow ministers to have far greater ownership of policy. Although, as some were to find out later, Latham and his office were more than capable of deciding policy for them.

There was another motive for decentralising the Opposition leader's office. Some of those in the shadow ministry who voted for Latham in the leadership ballot were wooed by the promise of extra staff. As the Parliament funds only a finite number of positions, the extra staff had to be found from somewhere else. Latham gave away so many of his positions that there was nobody in his office whose job it was to answer the phones. Mike Richards quickly came to the view that Latham simply did not have enough people to do the work that was required for the leader in an election year. His office was enfeebled, Richards believed.

By February—less than three months into the job with Latham—Richards was ready to resign. He believed Latham had no confidence in him. But he also knew that to resign would do untold political damage to Latham. After discussing the ramifications of leaving with John Faulkner and Simon Crean, Richards decided to stay. But his situation would hardly improve.

One of the areas in which Latham resisted advice—particularly from Richards—was concerning his relationship with corporate Australia. He often complained about having to attend corporate functions. He believed big business to be suspicious of Labor leaders. It was a suspicion returned by Latham. More than in any other recent federal Labor leader, there was in Latham an embedded dislike for much of corporate Australia. He considered that big business had been pretty tough on the Labor Party under his leadership. He believed this was undeserved and unfair because Keating's pro-business economic model that spawned Australia's economic success still lived on inside Latham's Labor Party. He also believed that too many corporate leaders, such as Victoria's Hugh Morgan, head of the Business Council of Australia, were blinded by their allegiance to the Liberal Party. They would never make a fair assessment of the Labor Party based upon its policies. He'd met Morgan and considered him a right-wing ideologue and a 'greaser'.

In early 2004, Latham was invited to dinner at the Yass farm owned by Rupert Murdoch. The dinner was arranged as an opportunity for Rupert Murdoch, his son Lachlan, and Murdoch's Australian chief, John Hartigan, to get to know Latham better. It was a strained meeting. Latham, ever the outsider, was uncomfortable around the Murdochs and seemed distant. When he foreshadowed Labor's policy to license a fourth commercial television channel, the Murdochs listened intently but remained noncommittal.

Latham believed he'd received no favours from the Murdoch press since becoming leader. He was miffed over the negative commentary about his intention to have the Australian troops home from Iraq by Christmas. This might partly explain an incident a few weeks later.

Latham was in New Zealand to meet prime minister Helen Clark when John Hartigan called his office to say that Rupert and Lachlan Murdoch wished to speak to him. As they'd just done with Howard, as a matter of courtesy the Murdochs wanted to inform Latham of a major announcement that would soon be made to the Australian Stock Exchange, the decision to transfer the News Limited's listing to the United States. Latham was in the air on his way from Christchurch to Auckland, so his office told Hartigan they'd leave a message on his mobile phone. When Latham retrieved the message in Auckland, he rang back and said: 'I'm not speaking to those cunts.'

There were only two senior business people in Australia with whom Latham talked on anything like a regular basis. Both were Victorians. Both were bankers. They were the Westpac chief, David Morgan—married to the former Labor minister, Ros Kelly—and the Bendigo Bank chief, Rob Hunt. Morgan was something of a private sounding board for Labor on corporate policy. Such was the relationship between the two that Latham assumed that Morgan would tell him when Labor was doing wrong.

Latham's testy, distant relationship with business wasn't helped when early into his leadership he met some of the country's most powerful bosses. In March 2004, he was asked to a private dinner in Sydney with corporate chiefs including Commonwealth Bank head David Murray, Wesfarmers' Michael Chaney and Hugh Morgan, organised by the Business Council of Australia. When Latham arrived at the appointed time of 6.30 pm, there was no one to meet him. The corporate heads were in a strategy meeting. They left Latham waiting in a reception room for fifteen minutes. He thought this treatment cavalier and was petulant and disengaged throughout dinner. Although the dinner meeting was supposed to have been conducted under Chatham House Rules—what is said inside stays inside—the *Financial Review*'s Chanticleer column later that week carried an account from inside that was unflattering to Latham: Latham had given Michael Chaney short shrift on industrial relations and wasn't receptive to the business chiefs support for a greatly expanded migration program. The leak caused Latham's office to formally complain to the Business Council.

At about this time Paul Keating started making frequent phone calls to Latham, increasing in number as the election campaign approached. Latham's staff believed Keating had two messages: to get the economic achievements of the Hawke-Keating era into the public debate, and for Latham to follow his own instincts, not the course urged upon him by the Labor

Party machine. Keating had supported Latham's bid for the leadership, telling him just before the vote that he should find his own way to take the Labor Party forward.

And like Keating, who had spectacularly fallen out with Labor's headquarters in his disastrous 1996 campaign, the fallouts between Latham and those who advised him would only intensify once the election campaign began. His own instincts would be paramount.

Chapter 9

The Death of the Grand Design

HIGH SUMMER'S CRACKLING ENTHUSIASM AROUND MARK Latham flickered when staff heard him yelling at his economic advisor and friend, Alex Sanchez. It was the office's first stand-up row since Latham had become leader six weeks before. The language from both was choice. Sanchez, a handsome man of Spanish descent, had no qualms about giving as good as he got from Latham. Advisors, who had come into the Sydney office from holidays to prepare for Labor's national conference, froze. Behind the exchange lay Latham's push for a radical tax policy that would slash the top personal tax rates to 35 per cent. Such a huge cut—the existing top personal tax rate was 47 cents—would cost $10 billion. The plan also called for a moderate increase in company tax so that it would be aligned with the new top personal rate. It was audacious. It ran counter to the caution among Latham's senior colleagues, especially his shadow Treasurer, Simon Crean. It would infuriate the Left.

On this late January morning Latham was angered that a contract between the Labor Party and the Canberra consultancy Access Economics to design the policy had still not been signed. He was miffed that Geoff Carmody, the former Treasury official and Access Economics co-founder, seemed to be dragging the chain. Sanchez believed Carmody was worried about how Simon Crean would react once he knew of Latham's highly controversial scheme. He believed Carmody wanted to be fairly certain his project, once started, would run to completion. Latham told Sanchez to tell Carmody that he, Latham, was leader of the Labor Party, not Crean.

This was the dry economist in Latham at work. It was Latham the risk taker. It was Latham the political operator continuing a struggle with Crean—and much of the rest of the Labor Party—on economic policy. With one stroke, slashing the top personal tax rate would end the country's greatest tax avoidance scheme—that of individuals forming companies to cut their taxes. It would also meet Latham's desire, highly controversial within the party, to reduce taxes for vast numbers of middle income earners. He considered the high top rates a barrier to productivity and economic growth. Under his plan the new top tax rate of 35 cents would not cut in until an income of $75 000 had been reached.

Few people knew the detail of the plan, which had been kept tight within Latham's office, although one outsider did. That was Carmody, whose firm was seen by many as the alternative source of economic policy design to the Treasury.

The plan had had its beginnings months before, in September 2003, when Latham was shadow Treasurer. Paul Keating had come to him and urged him to cut the top tax rate. Keating believed such a radical and unexpected move would flummox Howard, who would not expect to be blindsided on tax policy. In 1985, when Keating was Treasurer, he briefly managed to align the top rate with the company rate and was widely applauded for the move by both the big end of town and by academic economists, who saw it as good policy for economic growth and to reduce tax avoidance. Keating had proclaimed of his move: 'At the stroke of a pen, I have rendered most of the Tax Act redundant and removed the incentive for tax avoidance.'

Like Latham now, Keating had been opposed by the Labor Left twenty years before on the issue of tax cuts. He had castigated left-wing ministers Arthur Gietzelt and Tom Uren, telling them with disgust, 'You couldn't sell ice-cream in the Gobi Desert'.

To pay for the loss of the revenues a tax cut would bring, Latham had his eye on some of the $30 billion that leaked from the tax system annually through tax breaks for business and the better off. Access Economics suggested increasing capital gains tax revenues, but Latham rejected this idea early. He knew that once Labor made known its intention of winding back tax breaks, it would immediately be portrayed as the party of high taxes. Labor needed to be able to offer the better off a tax cut. Designing a tax policy that cut the top tax rates—down to the level of the company tax rate—was one way to do it. In theory this would be good for the economy. It would lift the country's productivity because people could work longer hours without incurring extra taxes. It would divert capital away from tax minimisation schemes such as negative gearing property, thus reducing house prices. It would help revive Labor's reputation as the party of economic reform. It would brand Latham's Labor as a party concerned with wealth creation, not the old Labor credo of wealth redistribution. It could be the enlarged, inspiring economic story Latham would take into the election.

And Geoff Carmody was the man for the job. He had designed former Liberal leader John Hewson's 1993 *Fightback!* package in which the top personal tax rate was aligned with the company rate. By late September 2003 Carmody had put a written proposal to Latham for Access to research and design Labor's tax policy for a fee of $150 000. Latham's office was ready to go ahead then but Sanchez detected Carmody's reluctance to sign the consultancy contract. According to Latham's staff, Carmody was worried that Crean's security as leader of the Labor Party was deteriorating. What would become of the project if, say, Kim Beazley replaced Crean and removed

Latham as shadow Treasurer? Would the new team support such a bold tax policy?

Latham himself had fuelled the leadership rumblings when, late in September, he made a speech about taxes that upset many of his frontbench colleagues. He floated the need to offer tax cuts to people earning $80 000 plus—a figure many in his party considered high—as well as tax cuts for Labor's traditional lower-paid heartland. He did not disclose that he was already talking to Access Economics. One opponent who went public on the proposal was the Sydney left-wing front-bencher and Employment spokesman Anthony Albanese, who complained that it was no time for the Labor Party to be talking about reducing the tax take. Supporters of Kim Beazley used Latham's speech as a means of further destabilising Simon Crean. Even in mid November, Latham was still very publicly spruiking the case for tax cuts for higher income earners. He told a Melbourne audience that the top rate was a barrier to economic growth. 'If parents are raising children and they have a mortgage, especially if they are living in expensive cities like Sydney, Melbourne and Brisbane,' he said, 'then nobody should pretend that $65 000 is a huge amount of affluence.' There were those within Labor who wondered if Latham's brazen public support for tax cuts was calculated to undermine Crean.

By the time in late November when Crean had been told he'd lost caucus support and a date for a leadership ballot had been set, Carmody still hadn't signed. Latham, fearing Beazley would win the leadership, was desperate to lock his rival into the tax project. He wanted Carmody to sign the consultancy contract, ahead of the ballot. But Carmody wouldn't.

Following the ballot, Latham made what many in the party, including Beazley, considered to be a terrible mistake. He installed Simon Crean as the new shadow Treasurer. Latham had appointed yesterday's man to the second most important position in the parliamentary Labor Party. The blunder was made all the more obvious when Latham's willingness to heal caucus wounds meant that he could have called on fresh talent, such as Stephen Smith, Wayne Swan or Lindsay Tanner, all free of Crean's baggage.

The policy and philosophical differences between Latham and Crean, as might be expected from men of such differing backgrounds, were wide. Crean came from a privileged background. His father had been a minister in the Whitlam government. He was from Melbourne. He was an insider, a corporatist, a former head of the ACTU. He was process driven. Much that Latham wasn't. His approach to economic reform was to modify and add to existing structures. Latham was a renovator who'd start at the foundations. It seemed the only thing that united them was their loathing for the rival Beazley leadership camp. So why did Latham make Crean shadow Treasurer? The popular theory, though one never confirmed by Latham, was that it had been a condition set by Crean and his allies for their support of Latham. More likely, it was a misplaced loyalty to Crean on Latham's part. It was not a partnership that filled many with confidence, including Tim Gartrell, Labor's national secretary.

Crean was always distant from Latham's views on tax policy. He was opposed to cutting taxes for the wealthy. Cutting rates would have also reduced the windfall tax revenues the government gets from bracket creep—when incomes rise and people move into higher tax brackets. Crean had long seemed ambivalent on the need to return the proceeds of bracket creep as tax cuts. Indeed, there was evidence he was willing to spend the extra money as Treasurer.

Crean's views were understandable. As a former president of the ACTU, his instincts were with that constituency. He knew what was saleable within the Labor Party, which largely opposed giving higher income earners more tax cuts. And, as Labor leader, he'd felt the wrath of the unions on tax issues when he decided to support the tax cuts in the Howard government's 2003 budget. Although modest, they were dubbed the milkshake and sandwich cuts, Labor's Left and much of the union movement argued that rather than support the tax cut, the Labor Party should have said the money would be delivered to the people by way of increased spending on government services. It sparked a long debate within the party. At its end, Crean hedged. He said that under his leadership a Labor government would return the proceeds of bracket creep to the people—but it would reserve the method of delivery. In other words, Crean might use the money to provide extra services.

The hesitancy that Latham's staff detected in Access Economics' Geoff Carmody to sign the consultancy contract after Latham made Crean his shadow Treasuer was understandable.

A subterranean dispute that would drag on for months had broken out between Latham and Crean over Latham's enthusiasm for slashing income tax. It caused Crean to become troubled by Latham's tactics, led to a confrontation between the pair and ensured that relations between Crean's and Latham's offices were extremely strained when Latham succeeded Crean as party leader. It also caused Crean and others to question Latham's sense of what was politically saleable inside the Labor Party.

The clash between Latham and Crean on tax policy was sparked when Crean, as leader, discovered what his shadow Treasurer was up to. Crean had agreed to use Labor Party funds to pay for the research into a range of options for tax cuts, but believed that Latham's office had hijacked the study, narrowing its scope to the effects of aligning the top personal rate with the company rate. He called Latham in. They agreed, so Crean thought, to broaden out the study again so that other tax options, especially cuts for the lower paid, were looked at. But Latham's office continued with its instruction to Access Economics that the narrower option of slashing the top tax rates was still preferred. This time Crean went over Latham's head and spoke directly to Geoff Carmody. While he was prepared to look at slashing the top tax rates, higher income earners were not where his economic and political priorities lay. Instead, Crean told Carmody he wanted the study to concentrate on how and what tax cuts might be delivered to the bulk of wage and salary earners on lesser incomes. It was an entirely different brief to Latham's.

Privately, Crean had his own ideas for changes to the tax system. They confirmed the view that he was much more cautious than Latham. He wanted to retune the existing tax system—rather than embark on bottom-up tax reform—by keeping the top tax rate of 47 cents, indexing it to the rate of inflation, and pushing out the $62 500 income level where it currently cut in. He may well have cut the second top rate of 42 cents—which struck at $52 000—back to around 36 cents in the dollar. This meant, he believed, that most people would know they would never enter the top personal tax bracket. It would be an incentive for them to work harder to earn more. The Crean plan may not have simplified the tax system, nor electrified the aspirational voters, but it would probably have helped reduce the incentive for tax avoidance. And it would have been more saleable amid the caution and suspicion of wealth that existed within the Labor Party.

The underpinnings for Latham's far bolder tax reform ideas included his view that the Labor Party had become something of a rainbow coalition that tried to be all things to all people. According to some former staff, Latham believed that Labor needed to restore its brand as the party for people in jobs. And it also needed to provide incentives for people to return to the workforce. His tax reforms could provide both, he believed.

Disaster then struck in a leak of spectacular proportions. At the beginning of February 2004, Cherelle Murphy, a 27-year-old graduate economist who had left the Reserve Bank nearly four years earlier to join the *Australian Financial Review*, noticed a large yellow envelope on her desk in the newspaper's Parliament House bureau. Inside was a seven-page letter Geoff Carmody had sent to Latham the previous September confirming the agreed scope of Access' study. This was, the letter said, to work on the effects of slashing the top personal tax rate down to the 30 cent company rate. It was late in the day and Murphy, already under deadline pressure, skimmed the letter before going to a press conference. She soon realised the potential magnitude of the leak and was able to verify its authenticity with a senior Labor staffer. Her excited editors slotted her story for page one of the next day's paper. As leaks go, it was A Grade. Murphy had a document penned by an impeccably informed source.

The next day the *Australian Financial Review* ran Murphy's story on the front page. It laid bare the months of secret work in its first three paragraphs:

> Opposition leader Mark Latham is considering a radical $10 billion-a-year overhaul of the income tax system that would cut personal income tax rates and increase capital gains tax revenue.
>
> A confidential letter obtained by the *Australian Financial Review* shows the Labor Party has asked consultants to examine proposals to slash taxes for low and middle-income earners and align the top two marginal tax rates with the 30 per cent company tax rate.
>
> To help pay for the $10 billion annual cost of these sweeping cuts, Access Economics suggests abolishing the 50 per cent discount on capital gains tax for individual taxpayers, cutting multibillion-dollar tax breaks for businesses and relying on rising taxable income, known as bracket creep.[1]

Murphy also obtained email exchanges between Latham's staff and Access that made clear the preferred option within Latham's office was to align the top rates and the company rate at 35 per cent. This would require a 5 per cent lift in the company tax rate. Publicly, Latham tried to minimise the fallout by saying too much was being read into a consultant's letter and that no decisions could be made before the government unveiled its May budget. The tactic worked. There was very little follow-up of Murphy's story—until Peter Costello got hold of the Access Economics letter and flourished it in Parliament two weeks later. He told the House that the Carmody letter was no idle document and showed the Labor Party was actually planning to increase company tax. Things began to unravel. Latham, trying to head off fears about tax increases, gave commitments that Labor would not increase capital gains tax or company tax. These undertakings made it harder to proceed with the plans, though not impossible.

Latham's office made plans to go public in late April with the big policy to slash taxes. This would be shortly before the government's May budget. Latham's staff believed the Labor leader was enthusiastic about the early release of the policy as it would signal that the forthcoming election would be a contest of big ideas. Latham also suspected that Howard was planning large tax cuts in the Budget, and saw Labor wiping out the government's plans with its own big policy. He liked to think of it as the scene in the subway from the movie *Crocodile Dundee* when a mugger pulls a knife on Paul Hogan, who draws his own, bigger blade and says, 'That's not a knife. *This* is a knife.'

But inside the Labor Party, the Left was horrified and shadow ministers from the Right, including Crean, fretted over the plan's saleability, its scope and guile. They had their arguments ready when the details were put before the party's all-powerful Policy Review Committee in April. A PowerPoint presentation was made and care was taken to make sure there were no documents left behind that could be leaked. Latham,

Trade spokesman Stephen Conroy, shadow Assistant Treasurer David Cox, the leader of the Opposition in the Senate John Faulkner, Transport spokesman Martin Ferguson, deputy leader Jenny Macklin, shadow Finance minister Bob McMullan, and Family and Community Services spokesman Wayne Swan were at the meeting. Tim Gartrell also attended.

The grand design died in that room. One by one, most of Latham's senior colleagues set out their fears. The Left's Jenny Macklin was against tax cuts to the wealthy. Latham regarded McMullan as a classic tax-and-spend liberal so his reservations came as no surprise. Crean did not favour tax cuts at the upper ends of the scales and was also concerned about the spending effects upon Labor's yet to be announced health and education policies. Tim Gartrell called for more consideration. He knew Latham's announcement that Labor would bring the troops in Iraq home by Christmas meant questions marks were already emerging in the public mind about Latham's readiness to govern. The party could not afford mistakes in its economic platform. 'The view I have been putting is that the worse thing we could do is rush it and get it wrong,' Gartrell said later. 'One of the things Howard is trying to build up is that Mark is a young leader, inexperienced, and is not across the detail. The pressure is not really on us. There is not a huge amount of pressure for us to rush it out.'[2]

David Cox, a former government economic advisor, was the only one in the room who could be said to be philosophically with Latham on the issue. John Faulkner wanted Latham to succeed but may not have been in agreement with the proposals.

Despite the Policy Review Committee's hostility to the plan, some of Latham's staff pleaded that the project not be dropped. Within it they saw the foundations of the economic story that Latham could carry into the election: the big, bold piece of reform, a policy that would provide incentives for people to work harder and be well rewarded. It tackled tax avoidance but also made it difficult for Labor to be branded as the high taxing party.

But Latham told them the plan was no longer feasible. Perhaps he thought it no longer necessary to continue to fight with his colleagues over it. After all, he had lifted Labor to within striking distance of winning the election. The ACNielsen poll and *The Australian*'s Newspoll, both taken at April's end, found Labor and the Coalition in a dead heat— each sitting on 42 per cent of the primary vote. Still, some of Latham's staff thought he'd given away the big plans for tax reform too easily. They watched on sadly as, it seemed to them, Latham allowed Simon Crean's office to take over crafting much of Labor's economic policy. They believed it would be much diminished.

Latham maintained that the Access Economics study had been intended to equip the Labor Party with a matching policy if the Coalition cut the top tax rate prior to the election.[3] He did not portray it as his preferred option. However, his former staff insisted that it was.

A few weeks after the tax alignment plan was rejected, the government brought down its May Budget. Howard had decided to spend his way out of trouble. The Budget contained a mammoth $51 billion in new spending and tax cuts. It was more than double the amount of pork Howard had thrown at Kim Beazley in the 2001 election. Its centrepiece was to put between $20 and $80 a week in cash into the pockets of Howard's target voters. The money was delivered by a combination of tax cuts for middle- and high-income earners and spiced-up welfare payments for poorer families. Howard showered money upon families—those he most needed to ratchet up the Coalition's primary vote—by giving many an immediate, one-off $600 payment for each child. Another $600 was promised for later. New mothers were to get a $3000 baby-bonus payment—a match to Labor's previously announced maternity payment. The tax cuts were delivered by lifting the thresholds at which the two top tax rates cut in. The largesse was precisely calibrated: you had to be earning more than a $1000 a week to get a tax cut. Or you needed to have dependent kids.

Howard and Costello had landed the splurge on Labor's heartland—the aspirational young families in outer urban electorates. Latham, given his previous support of tax cuts for higher income earners, could hardly not support them in Parliament. But those outside the Coalition's target largely missed out. They numbered in the hundreds of thousands. Many were single. They were low- and middle-income earners. The question for Labor became how to differentiate its tax and family policy from the Coalition. And how to design a package that looked more kindly upon the lower paid but did not give Howard the opportunity to portray the Labor Party as financially reckless.

As soon as he saw the Budget, Crean decided that the centrepiece of Labor's economic package had to be delivering tax cuts to those earning under $52 000 who had missed out on Howard's largesse. They were the great hole in the Budget. It was Crean's long held view that these were the people to whom Labor should be directing tax relief. Latham now did not disagree and acknowledged that the Budget had dealt with some of the issues Labor had been working on at the top end of the tax scales.

Crean was heavily influenced by research from the Melbourne Institute, an economic think-tank that had done much work on the disincentives in Australia's tax and benefits system for people wishing to rejoin the workforce. He—and Latham—wanted a package that would contain an incentive for people to work. *The Australian* had highlighted the work disincentives issue in earlier research it had commissioned from the Melbourne Institute. Crean calculated that Labor could make an important ally of the newspaper with a revised, post-budget environment, tax and family policy.

Work on the package picked up over Parliament's long winter recess. It was kept very secret. Crean was so concerned about leaks that he didn't even trust the Policy Review Committee with details. Instead, he and Latham agreed that a pared down version of the committee would deal exclusively with designing the tax package. The members were Latham, Crean, Jenny Macklin and Wayne Swan. While Crean was no fan of Swan's because of his part in destabilising his leadership, he recognised Swan had to be included because of his shadow ministerial responsibilities.

Latham appears to have stepped back from the process of crafting the package in the wake of the April death of his big-bang tax reform proposal and the post-budget environment. He took a supervisory role. He saw his job now as one of listening to the arguments of his colleagues working on the package and of trying to guide them into making a well-crafted proposal that met the new objectives he had set out in his Budget reply speech. These were to broaden tax cuts to the less well off, simplify the system of family payments, and to provide a greater incentive to work by lowering the effective marginal tax rate.

There were probably several reasons why Latham did not pursue the big plan for tax reform. He told some of his staff he believed the February leak from Access Economics was the beginning of the end for the bigger economic story. It allowed opponents within the party time to organise against it. The leak also alerted the government. And he never had the support of his deputy leader or shadow Treasurer.

Then on a Sunday in early September, John Howard called the election. Latham would now go into the campaign without the brazen and inspiring centrepiece he'd planned. Whatever the truth of its abandonment, some of his staff believed this was the seed of a depressing outcome.

Chapter 10

Forty Days and Forty Nights

JUST BEFORE 8 PM ON TUESDAY 7 SEPTEMBER, AN AGING British Aerospace jet lifted into a still Sydney night and swung north for Coolangatta. The fifty journalists onboard the charter flight were covering Mark Latham's campaign and had been locked away in Sydney's Marriott Hotel where Latham had unveiled the centrepiece of his campaign, the Labor Party's tax and family policy. Most had been scrambling against early evening deadlines to finish their reports on the complex tax and benefits proposals. Now weary and hungry, they reached for a drink. The mood lightened. There was banter over the merits of Labor's tax package and anticipation of the week ahead on the campaign trail—Coolangatta, Bundaberg, Cairns and back to Sydney for the weekend. One or two younger blades tried to crack on to the female cabin crew. A male television reporter was at the edge of a campaign romance with a radio journalist. Ahead were five weeks on the campaign trail. There would be days of choking overload, savage editors, cramped hours on planes and buses, blurs of hotel rooms, booze-filled nights. Journalists lived for this.

This was the first long stretch of the Latham campaign.

The Labor leader had spent its opening days in Sydney and had then gone to Melbourne. He'd been privately disappointed with the quality of his staff's advancing—the venue selection and setting up of events—in the first week. He'd spent too much down time in hotel rooms. Tim Gartrell, Labor's national secretary and the campaign's director, was nervous about early glitches such as the lack of a Labor Party backdrop at Latham's first press conference. He'd complained to Latham's chief of staff, Mike Richards. Latham was deeply unhappy—however unwarranted—with some of his travelling staff. Big changes would be needed.

Everyone was feeling their way. Gartrell and his key assistant, Mike Kaiser, were coming to grips with Latham in campaign mode. In the back of both their minds was the terrible experience Labor apparatchiks had when working with Paul Keating, the party's last truly headstrong leader, in the 1996 election. Keating's staff hijacked the campaign's organisation, and there was a complete breakdown in relations between the prime minister and the campaign director, Gary Gray, who took to referring to Keating as Captain Wacky. Gartrell resolved that he wouldn't allow such a breakdown to reoccur. Latham soon tested him.

On the Sunday he called the election, John Howard signalled that the Liberals would make Labor's economic management skills their target. And he would strike at where Labor stood to feel maximum pain: interest rates. Labor, Howard said, was the party of high interest rates. He even put a figure on it. If interest rates rose under Latham to the average levels they reached under previous Labor governments, the average mortgage repayment would soar by $960 a month. It was a clever and lethal scare aimed at Labor's heartland. Australia's average monthly mortgage payment had more than doubled to nearly $1000 since Howard came to office and housing prices started rising. The figure for property crazed Sydney was $1300. Household borrowings were at record levels.

Kelly Johns lives at Wallan, an hour from Melbourne's CBD. On the fourth day of the campaign—a Thursday—she agreed to allow Latham and the media into the home she shared with her two young children and her partner. It was here that Latham was to take dramatic action to try and stem Howard's interest rate scare. Although he had been long wary of fighting Howard on economic management, he was convinced that the interest scare was doing early damage in the campaign. Gartrell, Kaiser and the Sydney Labor-aligned lobbyist, Bruce Hawker, had come up with a stunt. Latham would sign a huge cardboard pledge for the cameras guaranteeing that in government he would do all he could to prevent interest rate increases. Specifically, he promised to keep the budget in surplus. Kelly Johns' home was chosen because what the campaign strategists wanted most of all was for the media coverage to target young families. The family waited for Latham to arrive. And waited. He didn't turn up. There was no phone call to say why.

That morning Latham decided he'd not go to Wallan. Instead, he signed the pledge in the foyer of his hotel. It was not laziness. Latham's decision most likely reflected his reluctance to fight on Howard's ground. This exasperated his advance team, who never found it easy to convince families to allow politicians and scores of media to tramp through their home. It would be the first of many changes Latham would make to arrangements much to the frustration of Kaiser, who had worked for months crafting an intricate, daily schedule for the campaign. Latham also refused to do the second part of the stunt which was to brandish a letter promising to resign as prime minister if his government failed to keep the budget in surplus. It was, of course, the leader's prerogative. Keating had probably best stated the nature of the campaign tension between the leader and the apparatchiks in a curt letter he sent to Gary Gray during the 1996 campaign in which he complained that he could not tolerate a situation where his instincts as party leader held sway for three years, only to be usurped in the election campaign.

The unveiling of Labor's long awaited tax and family payments policy at Sydney's Marriott Hotel had come with a new Labor campaign slogan, 'Taking the Pressure Off Families'. It replaced 'Mark Latham and Labor: Opportunities for All' in an attempt to use the tax and family payments package to counter Howard's interest rate scare. The announcement was given a dramatic edge when journalists on the Latham campaign were suddenly herded into a large room in the hotel and told they were in what was akin to the annual federal budget lock-up: there could be no communication with anybody outside the room for an hour. They were then given copies of the policy to digest.

A number of journalists were put out that *The Australian*'s veteran political commentator, Paul Kelly, had been leaked the bones of the package and had run it that morning across his newspaper's front page. There was deliberation in the leak. In March *The Australian* helped fund research which showed the number of jobless households that could be reduced by changes to the tax system. This was the aim of Labor's package and the leak was intended to win an early endorsement from the highly influential Kelly.

At the policy's core was an $8 dollar a week tax cut for about six million people on less than $52 000 a year. The top tax bracket would be lifted to $85 000, and family tax benefits were replaced with a single, fortnightly payment. Its themes were help for the battlers, incentives for people in jobs to work harder and the offer of a carrot to lure some 70 000 jobless parents into work, which would be achieved by extending the tax-free threshold for the poor and by welfare changes.

However, the package also made some families on modest incomes worse off. This was, primarily, because Labor proposed to abolish Howard's lump sum payment to families of $600 per child. Latham tried unconvincingly to argue that the $600 was phoney money, that it would be eaten up by families having to repay benefit over-payments. The Treasurer, Peter Costello, quickly labelled the package as 'a hoax on the folks'.

As the package was being developed, Wayne Swan, Jenny Macklin and Bob McMullan had argued that the losers made it flawed policy. Swan believed that the low income losers in the package would poison it. McMullan drew up modifications but these were not accepted. Swan and Macklin did, however, succeed in persuading Latham to boost childcare benefits for those he expected to move from welfare to work.

The complexities of the package required hard selling, which was Latham's mission as he set out for Coolangatta during the second week of the campaign. When he awoke on the Gold Coast on Wednesday morning, he would have been pleased to read the view of *The Australian*'s Paul Kelly, who wrote that the tax and family policy represented the most formidable attack on Howard since the prime minister came to office. But Kelly also observed that Latham was of a sickly pallor and that his presentation at the press conference the day before was flawed.

Kelly was right. Latham had looked pale and ill. He later admitted he may have tried to do too much too soon following his recovery from the attack of pancreatitis barely three weeks before. He seemed empty, pre-occupied and distracted—the Latham marks of anxiety. Some of the travelling press wondered if the Labor leader was far more rattled by the campaign than they'd imagined or, even, if he'd resigned himself to an electoral loss.

Neither was true. Rather, Latham's mood reflected his feeling that the campaign had not come alive. He felt he was wasting too much time in meetings and hotel rooms. He was anxious about the reception of the tax policy. He'd had little direct feedback from the public. The old campaigner in him, the man who'd once planned Bob Carr's stunts, wanted to experience the rush and feel of being on the road again. It came later that morning, in the old industrial suburb of Northgate, about 20 minutes out of the Brisbane CBD. The Golden Circle Cannery was built in the mid 1940s. Its insides are winding, screeching lines of conveyors carrying wobbling rows of cans filling with fruit. The pallid, industrial green cafeteria is cooled by rickety ceiling fans. The factory has struggled to keep going, and this struggle was etched into the faces of its workers. They were mostly white and mostly sullen as they waited for Latham to come and talk to them about his tax and family package.

He strode in, sensed the stand–offish mood and appeared tentative and hesitant. Then, at a couple of tables off to one side, a large group of Asian immigrant women recognised the Labor leader and began to cheer and squeal. They waved and smiled and asked Latham to come and talk to them. Latham blushed, a smiled spread wide across his face, his back straightened and he dashed to them, his hands seeking theirs. His spirit was uplifted. At that moment the election campaign began for Mark Latham.

The timbre returned to a voice that had faded. The old Latham was back, talking about the things that had always mattered. Outside the factory he was asked at a press conference about criticism from the Australian Council of Social Service (ACOSS) that the tax package would leave thousands of families on welfare worse off. Latham replied: 'I have a point of difference when it comes to welfare policy. ACOSS is a welfare organisation and they seem to think we do people a long-term favour if we provide indefinite welfare support. I have a different approach in saying that the best life is not a life of welfare; it's a life of work. It's a life of endeavour and enterprise and lifting yourself up in life.'

He was blunt. He slashed at sacred cows. He confronted Howard on his own agenda. This was Latham being heard and at his best as a campaigner. It reminded those listening why he'd been elected leader ten months before. His minders beamed.

The next day—Thursday—Latham flew on to the Queensland sugar town of Bundaberg. His staff were apprehensive that busloads of Queensland National Party supporters were on their way to provoke a confrontation in the Police Citizens Youth Club hall where Latham was to speak at an open community meeting. But the only protesters who turned up were a group of polite middle-aged men concerned about fishing restrictions on the Great Barrier Reef. With his spirits up, Latham's humour returned. At a door stop outside the hall he bantered with journalists who suggested the former Liberal leader John Hewson was the true pioneer of the modern day campaign community meeting. 'No, Hewson didn't have questions,' Latham answered. 'He just stood there on the stage yelling at people and they threw tomatoes back.' There was even a schoolgirl moment—a reference to Paul Keating's 1996 campaign when he was mobbed by cheering high school students. The girls called to Latham from their school fence next to the hall, and he charged over to shake their hands.

Bundaberg residents thronged to the public meeting. It was standing room only. In contrast to the previous public meetings, younger people, some with children, attended. Latham won applause when he promised truth in government and when he outlined the tax policy's incentives for parents on welfare to get work. When the meeting was over, he didn't rush away. Instead, he lingered outside, talking with an elderly couple who had taken over the care of their three grandchildren from their drug addicted daughter. On the strength of that conversation Latham later announced financial aid for grandparents in such circumstances and personally rang the Bundaberg grandmother to tell her. With the return of his spirit and humour, he now added empathy.

In the spring sunshine, and with a slight breeze ruffling the leaves, Latham put his arm around Janine and ambled away. She was going back to Sydney. He was flying the two hours up to Cairns in far north Queensland. As he got to his car, his advisor Dave Britton quietly gave him news from Jakarta that would snuff out his hopes of winning the election.

Kim Beazley had expected Australian blood would run during the election campaign. He privately predicted months before Howard set the election date that terrorists would massacre Australians in the Indonesian capital. He believed the success of the terrorists who bombed the two Madrid railway stations in March, influencing the outcome of the Spanish election and forcing the withdrawal of Spanish forces from Iraq, would prove irresistible to Islamic terrorists during the Australian election campaign. But instead of the assault rifles Beazley expected, they used a suicide bomber.

At 10.15 am on Thursday 9 September 2004, Dr Harold Crouch, an Indonesian specialist from the Australian National University, was having a cup of coffee with Australian defence officials inside the Australian Embassy in Jakarta when the building shook violently. The rising column of smoke, a crater in the road and a blast hole in the embassy's fortified wall confirmed a bomb. 'The people killed were outside the front gate. It made a huge hole in the road and in the wall,' Crouch reported within an hour of the blast. The bomb had been placed in a small, silver Daihatsu delivery van that exploded as it slowly drove past the embassy. Nine people—all Indonesians and including the van driver—would lose their lives. More than 170 people were injured.

Latham knew little of this when he boarded his flight to Cairns that day. He knew only what Britton had told him from initial radio reports: there had been a blast at the front of the embassy and a fence had been damaged. But just after take-off Latham was told that a call had been received from John Howard's office. The prime minister wanted to speak to Latham. The Labor leader reached for the satellite phone onboard the RAAF Boeing 737 and was patched through to Howard, who was with his advisors in his Melbourne office. Howard told Latham a suicide bomber was suspected, people had been killed and that many more were injured, some very seriously. The government was sending Australian Federal Police and ASIO officers to Jakarta and Foreign minister, Alexander Downer, was readying to leave for the Indonesian capital. Howard agreed to Latham's request that Labor's shadow Foreign minister, Kevin Rudd, go too.

The scale of the bombing stunned Latham. The mood on his plane was sombre, and a feeling descended that the campaign had been returned to reality ahead of time. Latham's staff all shared his reflection that in the previous 48 hours the campaign had come alive and its momentum had started to build. Latham was doing the things he wanted to do in the campaign and he was relaxing into its pace, hitting his stride. As he flew over the north Queensland hinterland to Cairns, he knew that the best course was to suspend the campaign but he still wanted the televised leader's debate with Howard to go ahead on the forthcoming Sunday night. Latham and Howard later agreed to suspend the campaign until then.

That night in Cairns, Latham batted around the future of his campaign with senior figures in his party. All had wondered before the election was announced how the Australian public would react if such an event were to occur. Beazley was one of the very few who believed the bombing would do more damage to Howard than Latham. Labor had, after all, made a strong case that the region should be Australia's security priority. But Latham was pessimistic. He believed the bombing would cause people to move toward the incumbent—a view later confirmed in Labor's polling. Latham also thought that the Jakarta bomb would resonate louder than normal because of the horrific television coverage during the campaign's opening days of the brutal Beslan hostage siege in which 330 school children and adults died at the hands of Chechen rebels.

In Canberra, Tim Gartrell reflected that it had been fortunate that John Faulkner had suggested he meet with Senator Robert Ray and Faulkner's chief of staff, George Thompson, before the campaign to plan for the consequences of a terrorist incident. The trio wanted to avoid what they called another *Tampa* situation—one that might send the party leadership group into a panic. The structure for information flows and briefings to Labor's senior figures that they established during that meeting now kicked in.

Latham decided to return to Canberra in the morning. Elaborate plans to release the party's environment policy the next day, which involved ferrying the travelling media out to a reef and later visiting a tropical rainforest, had to be cancelled. Latham wanted his own reaction and demeanour to be seen to be above the skirmish of the campaign. He told members of his shadow cabinet security committee to be in Sydney on Saturday morning for a meeting to discuss the bombing. In keeping with the need for a steady, statesman-like approach that emphasised the national cause above party politics, Latham's advance staff were instructed to find two Australian flags with poles to be used as a backdrop for a press conference he would hold in the morning before he flew back to Sydney. They found them in the office of the Cairns-based Labor senator, Jan McLucas.

Before he went to bed, Latham called Janine from his large suite on the seventh floor of the Cairns Holiday Inn. They talked about the Jakarta bombing and the day's decisions. He told his wife that Howard's interest rate scare campaign had pulled Labor onto Howard's safest turf, and the bombing would mean the party would now have to engage with Howard on national security, where he was equally strong. He said the odds were now stacked against a Labor win. Janine agreed and said that from now on he should go out and enjoy the campaign. He should take pressure off himself by reducing any expectation of a win. This was a turning point for Latham. He now accepted the possibility of becoming prime minister was remote. He resolved to enjoy the rest of the campaign. He felt unburdened when he got into bed.

Latham gave none of this away when he fronted the media at his press conference the next morning. Dressed in a dark suit and standing between the two Australian flags, he said: 'There are matters that go beyond an election campaign, that go beyond party politics—this is one of them. The paramount priority of all of us in public life is to secure the safety and wellbeing of the Australian people. So it is certainly not a time for making any political observations or points.'

Geoff Walsh, the former Hawke government advisor and Gartrell's predecessor as ALP national secretary, believed that the Jakarta bombing could have been a campaign breaker for Latham, but instead it was almost a campaign maker. Latham had been required to strike a position after the blast that was both appropriate and relevant, even though he had no real role in dealing with the event. Walsh thought Latham demonstrated a side of himself that would not otherwise have been apparent. While Howard could have been expected to be naturally advantaged by the events in Jakarta, Latham's responses allowed the Labor campaign to recover quickly.

Polling by Labor headquarters showed that the bombing and the campaign's suspension did have a negative effect on voter acceptance of Latham's tax and family package. Before the bombing, 35 per cent of people were favourably disposed toward the policy and the numbers were building. Immediately after the bombing, the number collapsed into single figures.

Despite this, and his initial belief that the bombing would

favour Howard, Latham later came to the view that it actually reinforced Labor's regional security policy, which put defence in the region ahead of the rest of the world. He decided on a bold strategy for the resumption of the campaign. He would open his side of the television debate on a topic Howard would never have anticipated—national security.

On Saturday 16 September, the day before the debate and the resumption of the campaign, Latham went to a film studio in inner Sydney Chippendale to practise for Sunday night's television clash with Howard. A mock debating panel had been set up. Robert Ray played John Howard, and John Faulkner the Channel Nine moderator, political journalist Laurie Oakes. They ran through likely questions and Latham practised his answers. At the real debate there would also be a panel of press gallery journalists to ask questions.

Tim Gartrell had tried to negotiate a different format. He proposed three debates on three consecutive Sundays of the campaign with at least one debate held as a community forum-type meeting. This would have given Latham maximum television exposure. It was, of course, rejected by Gartrell's Liberal Party counterpart, Brian Loughnane. The panel of journalists—an echo of the first Hawke–Peacock debate in 1984—was presumably being revived by the Liberals to diffuse the impact of a one-on-one contest with Latham. The Labor leader had wrong-footed the prime minister so effectively before.

Latham was tense when he arrived at the Channel Nine studios on Sunday evening. He knew that for many viewers the debate would be their first opportunity to really notice him. Aside from being across his subjects, he'd need to display certainty, confidence, empathy, humour and even humility. And respect for Howard. He shook hands with the prime minister, who was standing at his studio podium, while a Channel Nine staffer began the countdown for the start of the debate. Knowing Howard was a lifetime supporter of the

St George rugby league team, Latham leaned across and asked him if he had watched St George get beaten on Friday night. Howard replied that he'd seen the game on television, then looked away in silence. Latham told him that St George had had a shocking start, that was why it lost the game and it was a tragedy the club was out of the competition. Still, Howard remained stone-faced and silent. 'Yep, they had a shocking start,' Latham added. 'But don't let that worry you tonight.' Howard didn't say a word.

Howard won the toss and was the first to begin the opening statements. It was immediately obvious to viewers that the prime minister was battling anxiety. He was having trouble controlling his breathing, his voice was uneven, and he needed long gaps between sentences to fill his lungs. He sounded wheezy and frail. Latham had been expecting Howard to either begin on the Jakarta bombing and national security, or interest rates. Instead he talked about Medicare—hardly his strongest card. The prime minister moved to both the economy and national security, but dealt with both in a negative manner by implying Labor could not be trusted on those issues.

Howard's breathing difficulties had the effect of making Latham more relaxed. He thought the prime minister was hyperventilating and he concluded Howard was far more anxious and nervous than he was. This gave Latham extra confidence. Like St George, Howard had a bad start.

In the days after the bombing, Latham had been careful to avoid getting into any political arguments about national security. He knew people would see it as opportunistic. He simply wanted the voters and the government to know that the Labor Party would be supportive of Australia's role in the ensuing investigation. By a stroke of great good fortune, Howard's deputy, John Anderson, had been interviewed on Channel Nine on the morning of the debate and had contradicted his prime minister by saying that Australia may have become a greater terrorist target because it had joined the war in Iraq. It was a line too good to ignore. Latham themed his opening statement on national security. He began:

> Could I just start by paying my respects to the people who have suffered so much in the tragic bombing of Jakarta. It's a reminder of the uncertain world in which we live. But I also think we need to be positive, we need to be talking about solutions and I hope here tonight that Mr Howard and I can show people the very best of our Australian democracy. After all, that's why I am running to be prime minister—to make Australia a stronger, fairer and safer place. How can we make our country safer? Well we need to do so much more in our part of the world to fight the scourge of terrorism. We need to identify and eliminate these terrorists. We need to break up and destroy Jemaah Islamia in particular. And this has been the problem with the commitment in Iraq. As so many experts have said, it's made Australia a larger target. It's made us less safe in the war against terror . . . so we can't afford mistakes like that in the future. We've got to get it right, get it right in our part of the world.

It was a confident, sharp start. And Latham stayed on top for the debate's duration. Channel Nine's electronic worm—which recorded the instantaneous reactions of the studio audience to what the leaders said—clearly had Latham the winner. The audience marked Howard down whenever the prime minister mentioned the war, but supported Latham's argument that it had made Australia more vulnerable. When Latham suggested Howard was not committed to serving a full term, the worm spiked upwards in agreement. Similarly, it leapt again when Latham spoke about his Medicare policy, the tax policy and education. Indeed, whenever the prime minister spoke, the worm turned down and hovered on the line between negative and positive.

The Australian's Dennis Shanahan, often cool on Latham, said in the next day's paper: 'Mark Latham won last night's debate on his delivery. He was personable without being mawkish . . . he has won for Labor and will provide a much-needed boost for ALP morale and a faltering campaign.'

Shanahan's fellow commentator, Paul Kelly went further: 'This was the best 60 minutes of the campaign for Latham's Prime Ministerial aspirations. The novice looked substantial and must have gained desperately needed momentum.'

Latham thought he'd done well. It was only as he emerged from the studio that a Channel Nine staff member told him that the worm had loved him. The debate was watched by 1.4 million people. He left elated.

Latham entered the campaign's third week personally recovered from the setbacks of the Jakarta bombing. On the Monday morning he went to Concord in the Labor-held Sydney inner-west seat of Lowe. Long an area of established Italian families, Latham walked the main street, visiting the cafes, patisseries, and bread shops. Some shop owners who saw him passing by, rushed out and demanded he come in. People stopped to chat. Latham was animated and his mood lighter. A bride-to-be at a dress fitting was charmed by the Labor leader. The normally reserved John Faulkner remarked, 'He's on fire.'

Latham used a footpath press conference to highlight Howard's reliance on his past record. He wanted to portray Howard as a prime minister who'd reached his use-by date and who dwelt in the past. Said Latham: 'For me, last night, the debate was a great chance to talk about Labor's plans for the future. I think the prime minister concentrated a lot on the past and, one thing about the past, it can't actually solve the problems that we face as a nation.'

By week's end and at the campaign's halfway point, Newspoll suggested Labor would make net gains on election day of eight to nine seats. It needed twelve to win. The poll put the Coalition's primary vote at 43.1 per cent and Labor's at 37.8 per cent. It was encouraging. It belied the ructions within the Labor campaign team.

John Faulkner joined Latham's travelling campaign team toward the end of its first week. The extended Senate sitting had kept him away from the campaign's beginning. When he caught up with Latham in Melbourne, he quickly decided the campaign team was in disarray. The relationship between Latham and his chief of staff, Mike Richards, had broken down completely and Faulkner believed that Richards no longer wanted and, indeed, should no longer be in the travelling party. The Richards–Latham relationship had been fracturing for months. And it was also clear that Latham's relationship with his communications director, Vivian Schenker, was strained. Latham had come to believe that she was too cautious in dealing with the media. Too often, he thought, her advice was to ignore them. In particular, this related to the period earlier in the year when, wounded over media exhumation of his private past, Latham reduced his public appearances. Schenker left the travelling party to work at Labor headquarters and help plan the campaign launch. In this new role, her energy and skills deeply impressed Gartrell, although he too had reservations about her ability to work with Latham.

Richards stayed on for a few more days. It was an uncomfortable time for him. He believed he was being frozen out. He'd find he hadn't been allocated a space in the staff cars, or he'd not be advised of meetings. He knew the end was coming when, one night on the campaign trail, he went to John Faulkner's hotel room to discuss a campaign matter. Before knocking, he heard Faulkner loudly talking about him on the phone. Richards lingered outside the door and gleaned he was to be told to go later that night. Faulkner did it over breakfast the next morning. For Faulkner there was no personal dislike of Richards, but he believed he needed to do what was best for the Labor Party.

Faulkner insisted to Latham that his travelling team needed

some tough campaign hardened individuals. He wanted the Western Australian MP Stephen Smith to join the team. Smith, a lawyer and former state secretary of the Western Australian branch of the Labor Party, is a fastidious man. His white shirts are always spotless and pressed. His shoes gleam. It is not a vanity but rather a studied attention to detail. Care with the detail was what Latham's campaign needed. Despite his own previous animosity toward Smith because of Smith's opposition to Crean's leadership, Latham agreed he should join. Two very experienced advisors, David Britton and Ross Neilson, also joined the travelling party. Britton was a former press secretary to Bob Carr, and Neilson had most recently been in charge of media relations for the NSW Police. Faulkner effectively replaced Richards as Latham's chief of staff and restored the crucial link between the leader and campaign headquarters in Canberra. Smith made it his business to ensure all went smoothly at Latham's campaign events. Britton and Neilson worked the travelling press and fed intelligence from the road back to headquarters. It was a very capable team.

On the last Sunday in September, Howard launched the Coalition's campaign in Brisbane Town Hall. Election day was two weeks away. He showered money. His centrepiece was $2.2 billion in spending on childcare with benefits extended to homemakers with children. Non-government and government schools got another $1 billion and there was close to $1 billion to establish a new network of technical training colleges. When Howard finished his speech, he had committed to spend an extra $6 billion. That was $100 million a minute. He also defied reality in his opening lines, saying: 'Australia should never be a nation defined by class or envy, but rather a nation united by mateship and achievement.' It seemed that if the nation wouldn't go along with him, then he'd overcome class and envy with barrel-loads of welfare for the middle classes.

Three days later—on Wednesday 29 September—Latham was also in Brisbane to launch the Labor campaign. His speech was still being worked on an hour before he was due to stand at the podium inside Griffith University's Conservatorium. Graham Freudenberg—the legendary speech writer for Gough Whitlam—offered his services to Latham shortly after he became leader. Freudenberg was painfully aware that a similar offer he'd made to Simon Crean had backfired. He'd written a speech for Crean, but word had leaked out and Freudenberg's involvement was interpreted by some in the press gallery as another sign of Crean's anxiousness. Keen not to advertise his hand, Freudenberg read through Latham's past speeches and familiarised himself with his spare style.

Freudenberg wrote the opening paragraphs of Latham's speech. The words seemed seamlessly Latham's.

My message today comes straight from the people of Australia. It's a message to the people, drawn from the strength and wisdom of the people. From the Australians I've been privileged to meet, across the vast suburbs and regions of our nation, over the past ten months. And the millions of their fellow-Australians they represent. Today I want to speak on their behalf.

I want to talk about opportunity, responsibility and honesty—the key themes of this great campaign for a new Labor government.

This message comes from the heart—the big heart of the Australian people themselves.

The simplicity and symmetry of the words imagined a decent inclusiveness. They made Howard's wearied talk of a nation united by mateship and achievement as empty as it was preposterous.

Gough Whitlam was in the audience and when Latham walked down the aisle to the stage, he rushed to embrace his mentor. Latham's speech echoed of Whitlam. He announced a new health policy for seniors. Medicare Gold offered no-cost hospital treatment, public or private, for all Australians aged 75 or over. It was free, universal and the costs were open-ended. But, in contrast to Howard's spending, Latham's package was more austere. It had to be. Labor had accused the Coalition of spending like drunken sailors and, desperate to fend off Howard's interest rate scare, it wanted to be able to promise a budget surplus bigger than Howard's.

The reaction of voters, however, disappointed. A Newspoll taken after both campaign launches showed the Coalition's primary vote had increased by three points to 46 per cent. Labor's had dropped a point to 39 per cent.

With less than ten days until the election, the Liberals now ramped up their negative advertising campaign. Two advertisements stood out. Both were devastating for Labor. The first was a rehash of an ad used by the Northern Territory Liberal Party in 1994. It depicted Latham as an 'L' plate driver and hooked into a troubling vein Gartrell's polling had picked up in March: Latham was seen by many as prime ministerial material, but he needed more experience. The second ad simply said 'Good luck' to those prepared to trust Latham with the country's economy in the light of his alleged poor record as mayor of Liverpool.

Gartrell and the ALP campaign strategy committee knew from internal polling that Howard's interest rate scare campaign was causing voters to leach away from Labor. The ALP's nightly tracking polling was showing Labor's primary vote in the doldrums and below 40 per cent. The Coalition was registering in the mid 40s and climbing. ALP campaign headquarters was desperate to break the headlock of the interest rate scare. It needed a big idea. A circuit breaker. The Sydney lobbyist and public relations guru Bruce Hawker had a good one.

He thought Latham should announce that if he won the election, one of the first things a Labor government would do would be to enshrine the interest rate guarantee. This could be done in two ways. Either Latham should say before election day that he would resign as prime minister if he failed to take steps to keep rates down, or he could promise to pass a law requiring the steps to be taken. In other words, the law would require a Latham government to keep the budget in surplus, and cut Commonwealth debt and federal tax collections—all designed to keep interest rates down. Hawker, Gartrell and Kaiser believed it would be highly effective because it was brazen and original.

Gartrell put the idea to Latham. The Labor leader would have none of it. He said he didn't want to be taken in by Howard. Labor would argue its case for being elected on its own terms, with policies for health and education. Hawker was infuriated. Gartrell thought Latham had seriously underestimated the interest rate scare. Confirmation came one week before election day.

On the first Saturday in October a large barbeque was arranged in Sydney's western suburbs at which Latham would speak. The Labor Party organisers invited families. There were balloons and jumping castles. Behind the fun was a deadly serious intent. Against the backdrop of a family event, the script called for Latham to talk to the media about the need to ease financial pressures on families and to show he understood that keeping interest rates low was of vital importance. Latham went to the barbeque. But instead of ensuring that his message on interest rates was heard, he killed it. Instead, he announced that if Labor was elected he would hand over the prime minister's Sydney residence, Kirribilli House, to charities for fundraising events.

It was a poor beginning to the last week of what had been a mostly well-executed Labor campaign. It would turn to horror. Hardly anyone yet knew it, but Latham was going to Tasmania to save the forests.

Chapter 11

The Black Forests

EARLY ON MONDAY 4 OCTOBER, TWO RAAF BOEING 737S were lined up on the tarmac at Sydney airport. Acquired in mid 2002, they replaced the air force's beloved but aging Boeing 707s, which had been used since the early 1970s by the party leaders during election campaigns. John Howard and Mark Latham had each been allocated one of the new aircraft. The press would follow them around the country in slower, older chartered jets. The demise of the big Boeing 707s meant that the campaigning leaders and the press no longer travelled together.

Had reporters been aboard Mark Latham's plane that morning, they would have seen frenetic activity. Latham was breaking for Tasmania. He wanted to announce his policy to curb logging in thousands of hectares of the island's renowned old-growth forests. Only his most trusted staff were aboard. Howard's empty plane was parked nearby and they were worried that the prime minister was also headed to Tasmania that day to announce his forest policy. The pair had been playing cat and mouse for weeks over Tasmania's forests and if Howard arrived in Tasmania before Latham, Labor's message would be lost.

The issue was hardly about garnering support in Tasmania. Labor was anxious to reclaim some of the thousands of its more socially concerned supporters who had been driven to the Greens in the 2001 election by Beazley's handling of the *Tampa* crisis. A plan to dramatically reduce logging in the Tasmanian wilderness would, Labor calculated, have deep appeal. The Liberals, too, had become aware that significant numbers of its mainland supporters were worried about the environment and opposed to the war in Iraq, and were toying with the Greens or even the Democrats.

Latham had been hoping Howard would announce the Coalition's forests policy first, allowing him the chance to better it. But time was running out. The election would be held in six days. Latham had decided over the weekend that he could wait no longer. It was high-wire politics Latham style. The dissenters, such as Mike Richards, had been shut out, information to them cut off. Latham's daily campaign schedule, usually emailed out late the night before to his key staff, had not arrived in the email boxes of some. The Labor leader's resolute faith in his own instincts had kicked in.

One of Latham's staff, who had rushed to Hobart to prepare for the Labor leader's arrival, reported back rumours that Howard was coming. Glenn Byres, Latham's press secretary, made urgent calls to journalists travelling with Howard. Other staff called Labor headquarters in Canberra. Nobody could establish before take-off if the Howard rumour was true.

The journalists on board Latham's press plane, also readying for take-off, were deliberately misled about their true destination that morning. They were told they were going to Melbourne. Latham's office feared that if word leaked out about his imminent departure for Hobart, the timber industry would have enough time to mount a demonstration. This would become the news, rather than Labor's policy announcement. Perhaps the name of the pilot of Latham's press plane should have alerted the reporters to the truth. Captain Green announced as they hurtled south that they were going 'to a destination that is a surprise'.

John Howard didn't go to Tasmania that morning. He went to Brisbane. He arrived at Sydney airport soon after Latham's plane took off. One of Howard's staff quickly learned that the destination on the load manifest for Latham's plane had been changed at the last moment from Adelaide to Hobart. Howard's staff guessed immediately that Latham was travelling south to announce his forests policy. Well before Latham's plane landed in Hobart, the loggers knew he was coming.

What unfolded in Hobart was the worst day of Latham's campaign. Forewarned, timber workers and logging truck drivers amassed near the Tasmanian Parliament. Latham was alerted over Bass Strait as to what was in store. A frosty Tasmanian premier, Paul Lennon, was waiting for him as were bolshie officials from the Construction, Forestry, Mining and Energy Union (CFMEU) and representatives of Tasmania's forestry firms. Latham needed time for a last attempt to persuade Lennon to support him or, at least, not to attack him before election day. His staff were instructed to hold the campaign reporters on the press plane at Hobart airport while he attempted to negotiate with Lennon. His staff were jittery. They feared a campaign disaster.

Latham's dash to Hobart had its origins in events that occurred just after he'd ascended to the leadership. The Greens' leader, Tasmanian senator Bob Brown, had written a letter of congratulations to Latham, inviting him to Tasmania to walk among the giant trees in the Styx Valley at the edge of Tasmania's World Heritage wilderness area. Within the Styx Valley are some of the world's tallest hardwood trees—mountain ashes as high as 25-storey buildings. The wily Brown leaked his letter, and Latham was forced to publicly commit to going.

Then, at the Labor Party national conference in January

2004, an unlikely little group formed to try and steer Latham their way on the Tasmanian forests issue. Kate Carnell, former Liberal chief minister of the ACT, who at that time headed up the National Association of Forest Industries, was at the conference lobbying on behalf of her members. She was joined by the Keating government's media guru David Epstein, Latham's best friend and Labor shadow minister for Primary Industries Joel Fitzgibbon, and influential faction leader and shadow minister for Transport Martin Ferguson. Also in the group was the timber workers' union representative Michael O'Connor. The Tasmanian timber industry, which Carnell represented, obviously wanted minimal change. So did the union. Exports were soaring and profits were up. But the industry also knew it would be impossible for a federal election to pass without both major parties having to acknowledge growing distaste by urban Australia for the destruction of Tasmania's forests. The industry and the unions knew they'd have to give something to the politicians.

The issue had been put on the boil the previous Christmas. The acclaimed Tasmanian novelist Richard Flanagan had written a powerful piece for *The Bulletin*'s summer edition, which was being widely talked about because of its eloquent exposure of the brutality of the forest industry's practices. Still, Carnell believed she could negotiate a forests policy acceptable to the timber companies with Labor's Ferguson and Fitzgibbon, and the union's O'Connor.

Latham went to Tasmania in March, soon after the national conference, and toured the forests with Bob Brown. This gave the conservation movement a golden opportunity to talk to the receptive national press travelling with Latham about logging in the wilderness area. In coupes to be felled, all the large timber was cut down and the rest bulldozed flat. The useful timber, mostly destined for Japan as humble woodchip, was removed. The coupes were then aerial bombed with incendiary devices and set ablaze. Following reseeding, 1080 poison was laid to kill the possums and wallabies that grazed on resprouted saplings. Other species, such as bettongs and quolls, were often killed as well. It was an ugly story the conservation movement hoped would disgust mainlanders into taking political action.

The pictures of an elegant looking Latham in a brown suede jacket surrounded by the big trees were compelling. Latham had not been associated in such a public manner with Green causes before and, prior to the visit, had had few dealings with Bob Brown. He liked Brown and admired his upfront style and direct language. Privately, he believed that Brown wanted to build their relationship because the Greens' leader thought Latham might well win the election and the Greens would hold the balance of power in the Senate. If that eventuated, Latham knew that Brown would have a political agenda well beyond forests and would lean on Labor for support. Latham also felt that Brown was getting close to the end of his political career and may have wanted to leave politics with the Howard government finished. After the visit, Latham was publicly, at least, noncommittal on Brown and the conservation movement's push for an end to old-growth logging.

But Latham had been moved by his visit to Tasmania—that is, the economist in him had been moved. He had visited a veneer factory near Boyer in Tasmania's south belonging to Tasmania's largest company and spearhead of the pro-logging lobby, Gunns Ltd. Latham thought it like walking through a museum. The machinery was old, no new skills seemed on offer for the workforce and value-adding appeared to him to be almost non-existent. Latham's speech to the workers long-hardened to the predictable words of the many politicians who had been through the plant surprised Michael O'Connor, who had called a stopwork meeting so Latham could speak. The Labor leader spoke movingly about the scourge of inter-generational unemployment in Tasmania's depressed areas. It seemed he knew much about it. The workers stopped shuffling and looking at the ground. They were, for once, listening intently to a visiting politician. And they believed him, O'Connor thought. Unknowingly, Latham had that day provided the fuel for the loggers' rage when they would later come to think he'd sold them out.

The bustling eastern Sydney electorate of Kingsford Smith is thousands of kilometres north of the silent Styx Valley and in 2004 it was an unlikely battleground for the environmental movement. One of Labor's safest and most comfortable seats, it is the nation's twelfth most densely populated electorate. Laurie Brereton, an architect of Latham's rise to the leadership and the silken-voiced headman of Sydney's best-known Labor family, had transferred from a long career in state politics to become the federal member for Kingsford Smith in 1990. By the end of 2003, many in the electorate believed his best days in national politics were left behind with the departure of his long-time friend Paul Keating, and that Brereton would soon announce his retirement. His wife Trish Kavanagh, a NSW Industrial Relations Commission judge, was recovering from serious illness. Some long-serving but relatively young local party members were lining themselves up for a run at pre-selection and were busily garnering support of local Labor heavyweights, including the NSW premier Bob Carr and former long-serving member of the NSW Upper House and Labor fundraiser, Johno Johnson.

Brereton had surprised both the NSW head office and his local branches when, in late 2003, he said he wished to 'go around one more time'. It was made clear to Brereton that he would not win pre-selection unopposed, although there was general acceptance that if a powerful figure, such as Bob Carr, quietly intervened on his behalf then Brereton would probably get his wish. But Brereton had another surprise in store. On a Friday night in June 2004, he made one of his infrequent appearances at a meeting of local party officials to say he was resigning from politics. The next day—Saturday—a hurried meeting of the likely candidates was called at Johno Johnson's home to discuss the pre-selection. They didn't know it then, but their meeting was futile. On Sunday morning Johnson took a call from Leo McLeay, the long-serving Sydney federal MP, who told him that Peter Garrett, the former frontman of rock group Midnight Oil, would be the new Labor candidate for Kingsford Smith. Johnson was astounded and told McLeay that he must be joking. McLeay replied: 'It's because the big boys have decided. Latham wants it and Garrett's been offered it.'

This was not the first time Peter Garrett had been duchessed toward politics and the Labor Party was by no means the first suitor. In 2003, Bob Brown had tried very hard to get Garrett into Parliament for the Greens. Knowing that the Labor Party would also be working on Garrett, Brown argued to Garrett that he should take note of the fall of former Democrat leader, Cheryl Kernot. When she joined the Labor Party, Brown said, she did not change Labor; rather the party changed her. Bob Carr had attempted to get Garrett into NSW State politics and Simon Crean also made overtures when he was federal Labor leader. Garrett was an attractive candidate for someone trying to shake the skin of the old Labor Party and cast himself as a fresh leader.

Garrett, of course, was no vacuous rock star. Midnight Oil had always been an intensely political band and Garrett, who holds a law degree, had in 1987 penned *Political Blues*, a thoughtful and in parts incendiary book which, among other things, lambasted the focus of western economies on sustained economic growth and looked forward to the day when an Australian government evicted the United States from the joint defence facilities on Australian soil. The Labor senator and Latham confidant John Faulkner had talked to Garrett on and off over the years about standing for the party and, with Latham's ascension, Garrett's interest heightened.

On a March weekend in 2004, the Latham family drove down to the NSW Southern Highlands and had a leisurely lunch with Garrett and his family. While Garrett's children played with Latham's older son Oliver and watched videos, the parents talked of Garrett's political journey, why he was now interested in Labor and about his views on the environment. Latham, aside from believing that Garrett would draw environmentalists and some young people to Labor, also believed that he had appeal in working class outer-suburban seats because of his edgy legacy as Midnight Oil's frontman.

Garrett and Latham also talked that day about which seat Garrett might run for. Nothing was obvious. It seemed that any choice would require the party to elbow aside a sitting MP or endorsed candidate. Roger Price, the Labor member for the western Sydney seat of Chifley, was one who gave the party machine short shrift when he was sounded out. But when Brereton told Latham of his intentions, Latham knew then where Garrett should stand. He insisted upon Kingsford Smith.

There was, however, a hurdle before Garrett could be installed as the candidate for Kingsford Smith: the Labor Party's National Executive would have to endorse him. Michael O'Connor, the forestry union official with the CFMEU, was his union's representative at the June meeting of the National Executive called in Canberra to endorse Garrett. O'Connor's presence was no accident. As a leader of Tasmania's timber workers, he had a long history of organising campaigns on their behalf. And he was already heavily involved in behind the scenes negotiations between the timber industry and the Labor Party on a policy for Tasmania's old-growth forests as a member of Kate Carnell's committee.

The CFMEU and O'Connor did not want Garrett in federal Parliament as the rock star had a long history of championing the forests. The union wanted assurances from the top of the Labor Party that the negotiations on the forests would be honest, have integrity and could be trusted. It won them before the meeting started. But O'Connor wanted no mis-understanding. He was seated directly opposite Latham at the National Executive meeting and promised the Labor leader that if Labor sold out the forestry workers they and their union would attack Labor during the election campaign. O'Connor then told the meeting that he would vote for Garrett because of the assurances the union had been given. He would later make his promise to Latham fearfully good.

In the first half of 2004, Martin Ferguson and Joel Fitzgibbon came to Latham's inner policy making sanctum—Labor's Policy Review Committee—with a proposal for the party's forests' policy that would end clear felling by 2010, provide an industry compensation package of about $100 million and lock up away about 4000 hectares of forests from the loggers—mostly forests unlikely to be logged in the near future. The policy was certainly modest, but it would have the backing of the logging companies, the unions and the Tasmanian government. Latham was unimpressed.

The Labor leader now got involved. He sent his chief of staff, Mike Richards, to negotiate with the Tasmanian govern-ment. It was a prickly task. Lennon and Latham were not close but Richards and Lennon had known one another for a decade and Richards also had long-standing contacts inside the Tasmanian branch of the CFMEU. Lennon had been a staunch defender of the Tasmanian logging industry, which he knew was the lifeblood of many small towns and hamlets in the north. Latham's ambitions were high. He wanted to lock up 70 000 or 80 000 hectares of forests. Predictably, Lennon told Richards there was no way he would ever support such a figure. Lennon travelled to Canberra later to continue negotiations, but what was put to him there was equally unacceptable.

The forests issue was the stand-off that marked the frac-turing of the relationship between Latham and his chief of staff. Richards' advice was sound. He knew that Tasmanian politics would never permit what Latham wanted. Latham accused Richards of being too close to Paul Lennon and the CFMEU. Despite Richards' protestations that all he had done was give a commitment to the Tasmanians to keep talking on forests, Latham sidelined him from negotiations on the forests policy. From the Tasmanian government's point of view, the negotiations became extremely difficult because they no longer had one figure from Labor with whom to negotiate. They had several.

Latham's frontbench colleague, the former ACTU president Martin Ferguson, flew down to Hobart to talk to Lennon and the CFMEU. As time ticked by and the election closed in, Latham's office became more and more anxious to get an agreement that Lennon would support. Other overtures to the Tasmanians came from Simon Crean, some by way of his brother Dr David Crean, a former Tasmanian Treasurer. None found a way through the impasse. Lennon would not support the scale of Latham's proposals.

Unbeknown to Latham, Lennon's office had obtained the results of Liberal Party polling—passed on by the logging industry—on how the Tasmanian forests issues was figuring nationally in the election campaign. While the polling did confirm that the issue was in the minds of voters, it was near the bottom of the list of vote changing issues. Lennon's office believed the Liberal polling and concluded Labor headquarters' own polling on the issue was ambiguous—a view that came to be shared, after the election, by many in the Labor Party.

The Liberal polling had, however, shown that for much of the year Green issues figured to a greater degree than in the past. In particular, the Liberals were concerned that Green issues were beginning to cut heavily in traditional Liberal areas, such as Sydney's well-off upper north shore. Many of those Liberal supporters being swayed by these issues came to be known as 'doctors' wives'. For them Green issues morphed with their strong reservations about Australia's involvement in Iraq.

After Latham's visit to Tasmania in March, Howard decided he would also need a highly symbolic Green issue to take to the polls—and the Tasmanian forests was it. That is why, during the second week of the campaign, he suddenly diverted his entourage to a rainforest outside Murwillumbah in northern NSW. With the old trees as his backdrop, Howard told the accompanying media that while he recognised most people wanted an end to the logging, ways had to be found to protect the jobs of timber workers. That set the hares running. The Tasmanian media carried speculative stories that Howard was planning an enormous compensation package to buy out the rights of forestry companies to log in 390 000 hectares of Tasmania's old-growth forests. These reports were not specifically denied, further spooking the Labor Party.

The night before he went to Tasmania, Latham watched the Sydney Bulldogs take out the NSW rugby league grand final at Sydney's Telstra Stadium. Shortly after 9 pm, as he was being driven home, he called Martin Ferguson. Latham told his shadow minister for Transport that he had decided to go to Tasmania and announce a forests policy designed to lock away 240 000 hectares of old-growth forests. A scientific panel would also be appointed to assess the value of those forests. Ferguson, who had been involved in the earlier fruitless negotiations with the Tasmanian government on the issue, was amazed. Latham had assured his most senior shadow ministers at a meeting in Melbourne three weeks before that he would not move on the Tasmanian forests policy before Howard. Their understanding was that once Howard announced his policy, Latham would go one step greener.

Ferguson thought the scientific inquiry was a Labor stitch-up and he warned Latham that Tasmanian timber workers would be deeply cynical about another federal politician coming down to announce what amounted to one more inquiry into their industry. It was the worst possible thing the Labor leader could say to the workers, Ferguson said, and the whole policy could backfire badly on the Labor Party. When Latham asked Ferguson to use his influence to calm the expected angry reaction of unions and dissident MPs, Ferguson said he did not have that kind of power.

That night Latham also called the Tasmanian premier at home. The conversation was brisk, as the federal Labor leader gave the premier a broadbrush explanation of the policy. Privately, Latham was annoyed with Lennon, whom he now believed had withheld information about logging schedules for various areas of forest. The maverick Tasmanian Labor member for Lyons, Dick Adams, who had opposed Latham on the forestry issue and Peter Garrett's pre-selection, didn't get his warning call until the next morning.

Shortly after arriving in Hobart, Latham met Lennon in the Tasmanian cabinet office. It was there that he outlined the full detail of the policy. Lennon was aghast. Latham said he would be announcing that Labor intended to lock the loggers out of 240 000 hectares of high conservation value, old-growth forests. A scientific panel would be appointed to assess the forests in order to confirm that they needed protecting. The great forests of the Tarkine wilderness, the Dazzler Range, the Blue Tier and the Styx Valley were on Latham's list. To compensate the timber workers who would be affected, Latham said he would be promising $800 million to fund new job opportunities in Tasmania and to modernise the forest industry. The plan was politically audacious. It was a very deep shade of green and matched the 240 000 hectares of forest that the Wilderness Society and the Australian Conservation Foundation wanted saved when Peter Garrett had been the foundation's president. These groups were Lennon's enemies. At his press conference, Latham was asked about Lennon's reaction. He delicately said that Lennon would speak for himself, but that the premier had been happy for Latham to come to Tasmania.

Flanked by senior public servants, Lennon had in fact fumed at the meeting with Latham, telling him the Labor Party would now lose two seats in Tasmania at the weekend's election because of the logging policy. Latham replied that Lennon was talking rubbish. He said Labor's research showed most people in Tasmania, as well as those on mainland Australia, supported locking away the forests. Lennon ended the meeting by saying the best he could do was go home and not make any remarks in public about Latham's policy. The loathing was mutual.

Deep Green tactics had worked before for Labor. The Queensland premier, Peter Beattie, had set out to woo the Green vote in the 2003 State election by spending tens of millions of dollars to end broadscale land clearing over a large swathe of Queensland. Farmers were heavily compensated. Later Cameron Milner, state secretary of the Queensland branch of the ALP, urged the same tactic on Latham, arguing that federal Labor could have a convincing national win if it promised to save the Tasmanian forests. Writing in *The Australian*, Milner said that any losses to the Liberals in Tasmania as a result of Labor's forests policy would be more than offset by mainland preference flows from Green voters and the leakage from those Liberal voters concerned about the environment—the doctors' wives. It was an attractive scenario, but it needed delicate negotiations with those affected and faith that their jobs would not be lost. Neither occurred.

Surly timber workers, goaded by the union, and logging truck owners with their convoys of expensive rigs were waiting for Latham outside the Tasmanian government offices. Michael O'Connor and other CFMEU officials had been incensed by a policy they considered an underhand, dishonest sell-out of timber workers. They also believed Latham's actions had trashed the assurances they had gained as the price of supporting Peter Garrett's nomination for Kingsford Smith. There was no quelling their rage. O'Connor told Michael Cooney from Latham's office to shove the policy up his arse when Cooney called to brief him. The ACTU president Sharan Burrow got the same advice when she phoned O'Connor in a vain attempt to hose down the union by arguing Latham's policy wasn't all bad. But the ACTU's federal secretary, Greg Combet, who also called O'Connor, appeared to understand the union's outrage.

Up until the time Latham announced his policy, the union had been campaigning against Howard in mainland timber industry seats such as those on the NSW north coast. The union's tactic was to persuade Howard that the electoral pain of a move on Tasmania's forests wasn't worth it. But its ultimate aim was to deny the Labor Party a reason to make big changes to logging in Tasmania.

O'Connor and his union now reversed tactics and savaged the Labor Party, publicly denouncing Latham's forests policy. The meeting of timber workers outside Parliament condemned Latham. O'Connor told the media it was clear Tasmanian workers and their families were being sold out to appease the Greens and The Wilderness Society. The next day's national newspapers carried pictures of forlorn logging truck drivers and their families. The reports said they were facing ruin. Dick Adams turned upon his leader, saying he was devastated and would not blame Labor supporters if they now voted for another party. Latham was being eaten alive by his own just five days before the election. Worse, the union snuggled up to Howard. The CFMEU launched a campaign in support of the Coalition provided Howard promised not to change the Regional Forestry Agreement which sanctioned Tasmanian logging.

This was *the* catastrophe of the Latham campaign and John Howard was watching it unfold on television with his advisors on the upper floors of the Brisbane Sheraton. Howard's office had been working for weeks on policies for the Tasmanian forests. The prime minister was under pressure from within. The NSW Liberal senator Bill Heffernan was pushing for his party to adopt a bold Green policy. Howard's office had developed several policy scenarios for the Tasmanian forests, ranging from minimal change to substantial. With Latham's policy announcement, Howard's staff rapidly began dusting off their plans and they opened a frantic round of telephone negotiations with the forest industry's employers and unions.

To set his policy well apart from Latham's, the prime minister wanted to go to Tasmania and announce a policy that was specific and did not rely on having another inquiry. He wanted to be able to give loggers certainty while gaining points with the doctors' wives for protecting high conservation value forests. He had a policy ready to go three days after Latham and he set out for Launceston.

Howard and his travelling advisors were unsure of what to expect from the forestry workers who had again gathered to make their claims, only this time in greater numbers than they had for Latham. Some had been drinking. But Howard won rapturous applause from the Launceston crowd of 3000. He was armed with only a modest industry compensation package—about $50 million—and the outline of a plan that he said could lock up 170 000 hectares of land from the loggers. Much of it turned out later to be either land most unlikely to be logged or land that was not forested. Howard received his loudest applause, however, when he said his policy would not require another inquiry. Later that day the unions publicly endorsed the Howard plan over Latham's.

Labor's fraught venture into Tasmania's forests was completed on election night when Labor lost the Tasmanian seats of Bass and Braddon. It was the beginning of the party's backwards slide.

Chapter 12

The Forces are Arrayed

JANINE, HER EYES RED AND RUNNING, MOVED AROUND HER husband's staff, talking to each of them, thanking them for their efforts during the campaign. She was gracious and lovely. Mark's mother, Lorraine, was sobbing and bewildered. A silent and ashen Gough Whitlam sat bent, slumped over a walking stick. Mark Latham was shaken, withdrawn, contained and struggling with his concession speech, telling himself he'd suffered bad nights in politics before this. He wrestled to steady himself for the inevitable, the long walk to the stage and the deathly feel of concession. Dazed staff trawled for long-gone hope and blurredly asked why. In a garish function room nearby, legions of confused Labor people who'd come hoping for a miracle had instead been swallowed in an apocalypse. Liberals were braying everywhere on television.

Twenty-four hours before, Latham and his campaign staff had gathered for a hopeful dinner, shuttered in the grand surroundings of Aria restaurant above Sydney's Circular Quay. On that Friday night, Glenn Byres had told Latham the results of the final pre-election Newspoll to be published the next morning in *The Australian*. It was unexpectedly encouraging.

While the Coalition's primary vote—at 45 per cent—was six points ahead of Labor's, the poll said preferences were running strongly in Labor's favour. The parties were neck and neck at 50 per cent on a two-party preferred basis. Latham was surprised, buoyed. It was a rosier result than the latest internal party polling, which suggested a net gain of four to five seats. On a great night, that polling said, they might just get a hung Parliament. Latham phoned Janine with the Newspoll results. Word got around the table. The mood lifted with the renewed chance of an upset victory. But Latham was cautious. He privately told some of his staff that he didn't believe he'd done enough to win the election. And he dwelt upon the damage that that day's handshake with the prime minister—which led most television news bulletins that night—might have done to his chances. It wasn't a good look, he said.

He rose to speak to his staff in the restaurant. Surrounded by Labor loyalists and with nothing more he could do to influence the result, this was a different Latham to the man they'd seen during the election campaign. He let his barricades fall away. He told them how he'd felt that afternoon, going back to his old primary school in western Sydney, looking up at the honour board to see his name and thinking how a good school could lift people up. This is what we do best, he said, going back to where we came from to lift up others. The echo of Keating in that sentence bounced around the table. Latham spoke of how one night during the campaign, a drunken businessman came over to his table in a Melbourne restaurant, yelling that he paid half a million dollars in tax a year and now Latham wanted to take money from his kids' private school. Latham said he'd never felt prouder of his schools' policy than at that moment—giving kids a shot at the title, rather than appeasing the greed and selfishness of an obnoxious drunk who earned more than a million dollars each year.

He said he'd just been told that Newspoll had the ALP at 50 per cent on preferences. We could still win, he said. He moved to the emotional toll of being away so often and for so long from Janine and his two little boys. His youngest son had been asked why his dad was kept away from him for so long. The little boy replied that the reason was 'poo'. The answer, said Latham, put his life in perspective. The only thing that mattered was Janine and the boys. He was still talking as the food arrived. A couple of staff lamented that there was no tape-recorder. They marked it as a very good speech. One or two even reflected that maybe Latham liked them after all. They could not have known that the last Newspoll was so wrong.

Now this election night misery. There was no hope. There were no grand surrounds. Dennis Glover, Latham's speech writer, silently rued his boss's failure to take the last piece of advice he'd offered: prepare a concession speech. No, mate, he'd been told. Latham would deal with it. He seemed not to have. He looked pale as he took to the stage. His were not words that offered what his party, stabbed and bleeding, needed most— hope. Even love. Defence of his policies, yes. The ritual thanking of staff—the list was short and pointedly selective. The now familiar road he'd travelled from Green Valley and the pledge that he remained true to it. An empty ending: 'Of course, tonight is not our night, it's not the night we were hoping for but I've certainly found the democratic experience is something we should all be grateful for in this country . . .'

The ordinary Labor people who'd come that night listened and politely clapped the leader of the Labor Party. They then shuffled off home, leaving behind half-full glasses, nibbled sandwiches and leaden dread. The Senate looked lost, and it was. Labor in Tasmania was gutted. Solid Labor seats, such as Holt on Melbourne's fringe, turned upon the party. Howard, ominously, won yet more of western Sydney. Labor had gone backwards under Latham, and was now holding three fewer seats than it did before election day. And the most hurtful of all, this fourth loss in a row gave Labor a primary vote of

37.6 per cent—even less than what it received when Howard toppled Labor eight years before.

There was one early, telling wound. Mortgages. Howard's interest rate scare campaign had cut Labor to pieces. Of the fifteen seats with the highest proportion of mortgagees, eleven had a higher than average swing against Labor. Holt was in the thick of this as the most mortgage sensitive seat in the nation, where over half the voters were paying off home borrowings. The two-party preferred swing against Labor in Holt was 6.1 per cent—three times the national average. The long years of economic prosperity on Howard's watch had created a nation of mortgagees. Many had borrowed up to, and perhaps beyond, their limits. This had been the first election to be decided by the ranks of the newly prosperous in the remodelled Australian economy; the economy that Keating had opened up to competition by allowing changes such as the entry of foreign banks, vastly increasing the banks' battle for a share in the mortgage market.

Latham shut himself behind the gates of his home that weekend. The family encircled him. His sister Jodi's big four-wheel-drive jammed the view down the driveway. Away from him, the examination of the defeat began. Peter Beattie said Labor should have run a more negative campaign against Howard. Michael Costello, Kim Beazley's former chief of staff and a former head of the Department of Foreign Affairs, said the Labor campaign had been a complete train wreck for which Latham had to take responsibility. Beazley was generous. He said Latham had averted the electoral disaster Labor faced under Crean's leadership. There was truth in that. The worst of the party's polling back then had flagged a complete routing— with up to thirty seats being lost.

In the days following the election, Latham's result would come to be seen as disappointing but no catastrophe. Labor had won five seats and lost eight. Certainly some safe Labor seats were now Labor marginals. The hysterics surrounding Labor's result belied the fact that it still had sixty seats in the House of Representatives. The Coalition had 87. The most troubling aspect for Labor, however, was the widening gap in the primary vote between it and the Coalition. Labor's primary vote—at 37.6 per cent—was historically low. It compared to the Coalition's primary vote of 46.2 per cent.

Latham did not reappear until the Monday after the election, when he went to the NSW south coast seat of Cunningham, which Labor had retaken from the Greens. He appeared restored and readily volunteered that the party needed to do better on economic policy. In Wollongong's Crown Street Mall, the Labor leader seemed bemused by those who offered sympathy and encouragement. Perhaps he worried that their solicitude detracted from his efforts to elevate the party's local victory. The sympathies were shared by many fair-minded people in the party who were prepared to admit the obvious—that the Howard years of prosperity were always going to be the boulder in the road for Latham. There was a sentiment that he had conducted himself well in much of the campaign and, if he learned to heed advice and become a more inclusive leader, then he might yet lead Labor to victory.

Bob Hogg, Labor's well-regarded former national secretary, writing in the *Australian Financial Review* on that first Monday after the defeat, neatly set down the feeling:

> Despite the election loss, Mark Latham clearly developed his skills and displayed his personal appeal during the campaign. He grew into the job of leader. Obviously he needed more time than was available to gain the confidence of voters . . . the next three years as ALP leader will give him the added maturity that voters want.[1]

Even that harsh critic of Latham, Michael Costello, continued to hold out hope that Latham could, eventually, lead a Labor government. Writing in *The Australian* the week after the defeat, he said:

> The number one question is whether Latham is able to acknowledge to himself that he personally was responsible for many of the mistakes that cost Labor this election and handed Howard control of the Senate. If so, he could build on the qualities he showed in comprehensively beating Howard in the debate and rattling Howard in the middle weeks to become a much more focused, effective leader. If he does this, Labor has a chance.[2]

Neither Hogg's nor Costello's optimism would last beyond December. Latham's inability to acknowledge his own failings would cause them to reassess his suitability to lead.

Eleven days after the election, Labor's parliamentarians limped into Canberra to discuss the result and to try and remake a frontbench that had fractured in the aftermath of the election. Crean, smarting from being sidelined in the campaign, had resigned as shadow Treasurer but fervently wanted to stay on the frontbench. John Faulkner had quit his job as leader of the Opposition in the Senate, saying he was sapped and needed to recover. The Canberra MP Bob McMullan claimed he was leaving the frontbench because he wouldn't be made shadow Treasurer. There had been a confrontation with Latham. The promising Victorian, Lindsay Tanner, would also go to the backbench.

After he'd resigned from Parliament Latham was unforgiving of both McMullan and Tanner. 'During the campaign, Gartrell and Faulkner reported to me that McMullan had been caught leaking against the party's best interests. I think people like that should go to the backbench and I told him so. Lindsay Tanner came to see me after the election and said that if I

didn't make him shadow Treasurer, he would go to the backbench. So I found him a nice spot down the back.'[3]

According to some, following the leaking of elements of
the Medicare Gold policy on the day of the campaign launch
and the last week's polling, Latham sought from Gartrell and
others in the campaign team a frank and confidential verbal
briefing on the source. Despite the difficulty of the task (skilled
Canberra leakers always cover their tracks) it was the view of
Gartrell, a number of McMullan's fellow Policy Review Committee members and others in the campaign headquarters that
McMullan was the source. In particular, they pointed to the
consistent low level of leaking throughout 2004 from the
Policy Review Committee group and McMullan's insistence
on backgrounding selected journalists about a big policy event
for seniors on the day before the launch—a request that was
flatly denied by campaign headquarters. Despite this, *The
Australian* ran the leak.

Gartrell viewed the briefing to Latham as highly sensitive
and confidential—the sort of frank assessment he had provided
to other leaders on request. He was therefore surprised to
receive a call from McMullan after the campaign in which he
informed Gartrell that he'd just got off the phone from Latham
and the leader had demoted him because Faulkner and Gartrell
had said he had leaked during the campaign. Gartrell rang
Latham to complain about both the breach of confidence and
protocol when it came to sensitive matters between the leader
and the national secretary. Gartrell was told by Latham that
someone has to take these leakers on, Bob's time was up and
Gartrell shouldn't have given him the information if he didn't
want him to act.

McMullan totally rejects the claim that he leaked. 'I invite
any journalist to whom I leaked to publish what I leaked
and I release them from their obligation of confidentiality.
Mark Latham didn't ask me if I leaked. He just asserted it. I
assume it was an excuse to get rid of me.'[4]

Beazley also elected to go to the backbench and adopted the House of Commons tradition of party elder-in-residence. Some saw a portent in this, his second early abdication. It was now obvious that the factions—which Latham had sidetracked to become leader—were reasserting their influence. Or rather, a bloody-mindedness. The case of Craig Emerson, the front-bencher responsible for workplace relations under Latham, typified their resurgent muscle. Emerson held a Master of Economics, a PhD, had worked as an economic advisor for the United Nations and was formerly head of the Queensland Department of Environment. He'd fallen out with his faction boss, the Australian Workers Union Queensland chief Bill Ludwig, for first supporting Crean and then Latham instead of Beazley, who was the faction's choice. So the faction picked Bill Ludwig's son, Joe, for Emerson's frontbench slot.

Latham had returned to Canberra defiant. He insisted that Crean remain on his frontbench, despite the resolve of Crean's own Victorian faction to dump him. And many believed that Latham wanted the young Victorian left-wing MP and lawyer Julia Gillard elevated to the position of shadow Treasurer. Beazley was one who was alarmed by the prospect. He went to Latham to try and talk him out of it. He believed that Latham could never be prime minister with Gillard as his shadow Treasurer. Costello would destroy her as the socialist would-be-Treasurer. In the end, Queensland's Wayne Swan got the job.

It was the saving of Crean that most consumed Latham. He was quoted by the *Sydney Morning Herald*'s Alan Ramsey as saying of the factional leaders who had turned upon Crean: 'Fuck it. If they want to take me on, they can and I'll just go. I've got kids to raise.' There was more meaning in those words than anybody realised at the time. They reflected Latham's immense frustration with the power of Labor's factional leaders. He had come to believe their self-interest was consigning the party to irrelevancy, preventing its reform, strangling it.

A deal was thrashed out to save Crean, whose Victorian faction continued to reject him. Latham had to expand his frontbench from 30 to 31 positions and he sapped his remaining political capital in the row. It was a Pyrrhic victory. Latham justified his actions by saying Labor owed respect to former leaders.

At the party's first post-election party room meeting, Latham allowed the critics full vent. Mostly, however, they were muted by the dread of worsening their party's public agony. Equipped with head office polling, Latham argued the Liberals' expensive bombardment of negative advertising had cruelled the gains Labor had been making in the campaign with its policy announcements. He said Howard's interest rate scare had broken through in the campaign's last week. Latham's leadership was not challenged, yet his need to stare down the factions so soon after the defeat unmasked the brittleness of the party's hastily erected facade of recovery.

Meanwhile, the debate within the party over the election result was gathering pace. The disparity of views was best illustrated by the thoughts of two of the party's thinkers—one an elder, the other a rising influence. Barry Jones, writing for *The Age* in his capacity as the Labor Party's senior vice-president, lamented Labor's abandonment of the Left, which he defined as those people who believed that the world should be improved. Instead, voters were given a choice between two conservative parties—tantamount to having to choose between McDonald's and KFC, Jones wrote. He said Labor had been light in too many policy areas: the arts, Aborigines, refugees, water, foreign affairs, women, the third age, the ABC, science, population and migration, trade and industry, and industrial relations.

In contrast to Barry Jones' views, Bill Shorten, the young Victorian lawyer and national secretary of the Australian Workers Union, wrote in an article for the Fabian Society that Labor's big 'L' left appeals meant that the party had vacated the centre ground, leaving it for John Howard to exploit. Labor released too many policies, he said, while the Coalition stuck to a few key messages. Jones and Shorten agreed on one thing, however: Labor's failure to establish its economic credentials.

On 23 November, Latham went to Labor's headquarters in Canberra to address the National Executive—the party's supreme governing body which is dominated by union leaders. He was there to speak about the election result.

The National Executive had reports before it commissioned by Labor's head office to critique the campaign, the party's polling and the policies Latham took to the election. Graeme Wedderburn, Bob Carr's chief of staff, wrote the report on policies. He took issue with the tax and family package. There shouldn't have been losers, he said: 'With cumulative budget surpluses of $25 billion revealed during the campaign, there was room for winners and almost no reason for losers.'

Wedderburn's report also questioned the central theme of Latham's schools policy, which was to take money from wealthy private schools. Labor should consider, he said, 'challenging the notion that education policy should have as its focus a revival of State funding arguments for private schools when a large and increasing number of people are choosing non-government schools for their children'.

There was also a report highly critical of the manner in which advertising space was bought for the party during the campaign. Written by Cameron Milner, the former state secretary of the Queensland ALP, the report said radio advertising was heavily under used, and slots around radio and television news bulletins were not bought for Labor advertising despite a clear directive from the Labor campaign team. Milner concluded there had been failures in the planning stages of the Labor media campaign.

The atmosphere was querulous in the ALP conference room when Latham took his seat in the middle of the big rectangular table. Bill Shorten sat directly opposite and pulled out a pad and pen, ready to take notes of Latham's words. He had deliberately placed himself next to Scott McLean of the Construction, Forestry, Mining and Energy Union (CFMEU) in case Latham went on the attack over the CFMEU's campaign against his Tasmanian forests policy. Shorten intended to come to McLean's defence. The room was tense but there was a willingness to give Latham a fair hearing. What followed, however, antagonised many members of the National Executive, Latham's parliamentary colleagues and the Labor premiers.

Latham said he'd seen a lot of opinion about the reasons for the election result. He'd read both Shorten's and Barry Jones' views. Both were horseshit, he said. People needed to understand that the old Left and Right divides no longer mattered. Latham then cited his list of reasons for the result. They included actions by both the NSW and Victorian state governments that drove down Labor's vote. For NSW, he mentioned the row in western Sydney over the closure of the Orange Grove retail site. In Victoria, it was the controversy of the Mitcham–Frankston motorway toll. The Tasmanian Labor government had derailed his forests policy by withholding its cooperation and he'd been let down by some of his staff. Head office was not spared. Latham rounded upon the quality of the party's campaign advertising and what he called a lack of counter-offensive measures against the Coalition's tactics. He said the advertisements prepared by Labor headquarters to respond to Liberal advertising were too little, too late.

Those present were said to be angered that Latham seemed to admit little fault himself. All held their tongues. But many did agree with Latham's analysis that the Labor Party's caucus was now divided into multiple sub-factions and personal fiefdoms. He was said to have posed the rhetorical question: Does the party need a leader or telephone receptionist?

After this, Bob Hogg and Michael Costello turned upon Latham in their influential newspaper columns. Hogg wrote that he too had shared in the welter of self-denial about the defeat, but the goodwill extended to Latham in the hope he would develop into a long-term leader had been misplaced. Hogg said he agreed with Latham's view about the fracturing of the caucus into fiefdoms, but concluded the party needed a new leader to unite it. Costello was blunter. He said Latham could not bring himself to say, without qualification, that he was responsible for the election result. He was now Monty Python's dead parrot.

The generous voice of Graham Freudenberg, Whitlam's former speech writer, was one of the few to publicly come to Latham's defence. Freudenberg called upon the party to give the leader the space he needed. He asked it to acknowledge that Latham's re-election as leader, unopposed after the election loss, was a decision for the long haul. The party had not taken Latham on sufferance, Freudenberg said. He added that Latham needed to openly adopt a two-term re-election strategy.

Latham, however, appeared not to help his case by exacerbating a very public brawl he was having with the Victorian senator and Beazley supporter, Stephen Conroy, whom Latham suspected was campaigning within the party to undermine his leadership. Latham believed his old enemies—the factional leaders who'd wanted Beazley instead of him, some unionists on the party's national executive and state officeholders—were re-grouping.

He thought Conroy was doing 'Business as usual—leaking, undermining, destabilising, just as he had done for two years with Crean'. Latham believed Conroy had leaked unflattering material about his leadership to the *Australian Financial Review*, and that his actions were symptomatic of wider activity within the party against him. He came to believe that there were powerful people in the Labor Party who had set out to end his leadership.

It is important to remember that when I won the [leadership] ballot in December 2003, dozens of machine-men in the party backed Beazley. Go through the list of so-called power-brokers and union leaders. They do not like a parliamentary leader who refuses to wobble like a big piece of jelly. They like someone who is compliant to the interests of the faction chiefs, union bosses and State-based machines. And they do not like to lose.

When Crean took on organisational reform of the party after our 2001 defeat, they organised against him. After I lost in 2004, it was my turn. Finally in 2005 the machine men got their man, Beazley, back into the job. It's not a matter of Left or Right. It's the exertion of machine control over the Federal Labor Party. Whatever it takes.[5]

Latham believed that the buoyant economy ensured Howard's election win. According to him, Labor's internal polling showed that throughout 2004 a large majority of Australians thought the country was headed in the right direction because of the more than decade-long streak of strong economic growth. 'There is no history in Australia of Governments being defeated in these circumstances. We put forward a number of social issues and policies that had positive impact, but not enough to overcome the government's advantage on the economy.[6]

Soon after the election, Latham formed the view that he'd been badly let down by Labor headquarters. He believed campaign director, Tim Gartrell, had failed to effectively counter the Liberals' advertising designed to fuel fears of rising interest rates under Labor. Latham was incredulous that it took two weeks to produce a single advertisement to counter the Liberals' interest rates blitz. He believed this to be a miserable effort—particularly as Labor headquarters had long expected the Liberals to use the tactic and because he'd been making himself available for the filming of advertising material since May. He believed Labor's response advertisements should have been ready to air before the campaign started.

How Labor failed to defeat Howard's interest rate scare would become the deepest rift between Latham and Labor headquarters, as would the bitter feud over how campaign headquarters responded to the Liberals' use of Latham's record as mayor of Liverpool Council.

The differences were stark.

Tim Gartrell believed that Latham did not want to be drawn into what he (Latham) termed Howard's issues—such as the economy and interest rates. Similarly, Gartrell believed Latham ruined efforts by Labor headquarters and others to hit back at Howard's attempt to use his record at Liverpool Council against Labor. Latham contended to Gartrell that the Liverpool issue had already been dealt with.

In late May 2004—four months before the election—Gartrell and other members of Labor's campaign strategy group dined with Latham at the Waters Edge restaurant in Canberra. The group wanted to brief Latham on the attacks they expected the Liberals to mount during the campaign. Mike Kaiser, Gartrell's right-hand man, had drawn up a risk assessment and mitigation table—a document that was shown to Latham at the dinner. As its title suggests, it set down campaign risks for Latham and the means of countering them. The prospect of a scare campaign on interest rates topped Kaiser's list. According to some of those present, Latham agreed with both the risk and the mitigation side of the document.

A month before that dinner, the likelihood of a Liberal threat on interest rates and on Latham's Liverpool Council record had been at the forefront of a mock election campaign held at Labor's Canberra headquarters on 29–30 April 2004.

Risk Assessment and Mitigation

Risk	Mitigation
Labor can't be trusted to manage the economy, interest rates	• Surround ML with a 'council of elders' • 'Trilogy' style pledge • Have a 3rd Party say 'expect no different approach to fiscal rectitude under Labor' • Prosperity with a purpose—economy may be going well, but families aren't feeling the pay-off
Labor is a risk to National Security/ US alliance/soft on refugees	• Stop talking about it unless we're dragged there • Howard's practical failing, eg airport security, Brigitte, Collins • Troops needed at home—parochial appeal • 3rd party commentary to reinforce above
ML lacks experience, he's a risk	• ML has 'relevant experience' (one of us, family, suburbia) • He understands problems and wants to fix them • ML's experienced enough to make an impact from opp'n eg pollie super • Govt, PM tired, old ideas • Tell ML's life story—Qualifications, Party, Degree, Council, books/ideas
The Govt's tax cut	• Pre-empt with campaign on cost of living increases and tax increases • Labor's alternate proposition (mix of tax cut and services?)
Labor/ ML's not ready	• Compelling reasons to change • Language: before it's too late/while we can • Howard's only sticking around for the record books • Emphasise the policy work that's occurred in opposition • 3rd party commentary

Involving seventy people, its purpose was to familiarise campaign staff with Labor headquarters and to simulate random campaign events so that weaknesses within the Labor team could be identified. The exercise was codenamed SimCity Tornado—after the computer game that allows players to set disasters upon a large city. The Canberra simulation threw a number of testing scenarios at Labor's campaign policy and media units—including a Liberal scare campaign on interest rates and on Latham's time at Liverpool Council.

By August, Labor's focus group polling in Sydney's mortgage belt seats was ringing alarm bells on interest rates. The issue eclipsed virtually everything. The NSW Branch secretary, Mark Arbib, and Laurie Brereton met with Latham on 12 August. Arbib warned Latham that the Liberals would run an interest rates scare campaign. He said Latham now needed to confront the issue by talking about interest rates and economic management. And he needed to make public statements that urged a hold on rates each time the Reserve Bank board met. Brereton agreed with Arbib's views. Less than three weeks later Howard called the election and opened the Liberal campaign with the question: 'Who do you trust to keep interest rates low?'

His fears confirmed, Gartrell directed Labor's advertising agencies to immediately begin work on producing advertisements in response to the interest rate scare. But the agencies were having serious trouble. None of their ads were working. Very early in the election year a series of negative advertisements attacking John Howard were tested. Most were rejected by focus groups. One early advertisement depicted Howard as the battery-powered Duracell man who, after a spurt of frenetic activity, ran out of puff. It failed because the focus groups said Howard did indeed look like the Duracell man during his often televised walks, but he never ran out of puff. It took five months to find a negative Howard advertisement that worked. It said John Howard always blamed others for his government's mistakes.

The first set of ads tested employed expert commentary from financial specialists who explained that interest rates were little influenced by the party that was in government. The focus groups rejected the message. They instead responded that they remembered how high interest rates were in the Hawke–Keating era. Alarmingly, their recall of that era, when rates reached 17 per cent, was immediate.

Gartrell decided he could not waste precious advertising dollars on ads that were not going to work. He and the advertising agencies began trying other concepts to fight off the Liberals' interest rate scare. Nothing worked. It was not until late September, in the election campaign's final stages, that they had something to work with. A Reuters poll of fourteen market economists had found them in agreement that whoever won the election would make no difference to interest rates over the next three years. A script was put together around the poll's findings. Labor's campaign strategists were desperate. They knew the Liberals' interest rate scare was killing the Labor campaign. Labor's advertisement asked people whom they believed on interest rates: John Howard or the fourteen market economists? It concluded: 'John Howard will say anything to get elected. He's unbelievable.'

On 29 September, after Labor's Brisbane campaign launch, Gartrell went to Latham's hotel room and tried to persuade the Labor leader to take up Bruce Hawker's idea and now say publicly that if elected he would pass a law to enshrine his interest rate guarantee. A second option was to say he'd resign as prime minister if he broke the pledge. Latham refused. Despite Latham's view that Labor should undertake no more interest rate stunts or campaign on what he called Howard's issues, Gartrell put the Labor Party's interest rate advertisement to air. It quoted the fourteen market economists and the former Reserve Bank governor, Bernie Fraser, dismissing the Liberal scare campaign as nonsense. Gartrell poured much of the advertising money he had left into blitzing the 30 second advertisement. Of course, it was too late. Gartrell's heart sank when he saw the results of Labor's quantitative polling conducted over the three nights out from election day. A majority of swinging voters responded that even though they believed it was time to change the government, they couldn't take the slightest risk that their interest rates would rise.

Six months out from the election campaign, Gartrell made some interesting conclusions about his dealings with Latham and the reasons for the election loss.

Despite his reputation as a hothead and his tendency towards running a one-man band, I always found Latham good to deal with—accessible, committed and always thinking tactically about the immediate events. He was a skilled tactician, something Howard underestimated during times like the debate over the US Free Trade Agreement. He was strongly dedicated to winning—very hungry for it.

Mark had a strong view about our campaign. On numerous occasions he made it clear—he wanted a positive campaign focused on our issues. He didn't want to be seen as oppositionist or carping. He adopted the title Labor leader instead of leader of the Opposition. He didn't want to campaign on 'their issues'. Early in 2004 he even canvassed the possibility of us running no negative ads.

This worked brilliantly for the first six months of his leadership and he enjoyed an unprecedented honeymoon.

With the all powerful benefit of hindsight, that left us massively exposed on 'their issues'—the economy, particularly interest rates, and which leader had the experience to govern. This meant it was left to the campaign to advance a range of arguments—our positive agenda, our leader's credentials, their poor record on health, education and family payments as well as inoculate against their attacks on Mark's record on Liverpool Council and Labor's legacy on interest rates. All this with at least $3 million less in the kitty for ads.[7]

On 24 August 2004—about a week before the election was called—the Labor leader met with Gartrell. He told Labor's federal secretary he'd read Sidney Blumenthal's *The Clinton Wars*, a towering book on Clinton's years in the Oval Office, and had been left with the impression that rapid response was critical in election campaigns. Gartrell knew that rapid response strategies had been part of Labor campaigns for a decade. Rapid response would form the bulk of the work of the media and policy units that would be established once Howard called the election. Latham later recalled that meeting:

> Prior to the campaign, I asked Gartrell to make sure that we had a rapid response and rebuttal operation in place to deal with Liberal propaganda. It was obvious that they were going to go hard in the media and very negative in their advertising. Gartrell assured me that campaign headquarters would rebut everything straight away; although his assessment was that their negative attack on the economy would be directed towards Crean. This didn't actually happen. I have diary notes that record the detail of this conversation on August 24.
>
> My job during the campaign was to do policy announcements and media interviews on the road. I didn't have time to watch television and see the ads, let alone devise and produce our ad campaign. That was the responsibility of the campaign director. I did not veto any ads. In fact the only time I saw a series of draft ads was in the second last week and that was mainly for information purposes.[8]

In an email in early April 2005, Latham provided a fuller account of what he believed were the failings of Labor's campaign headquarters.

> At the first Caucus meeting after the election (so this is no great secret), I reported to the colleagues John Faulkner's advice to me

on the polling during the campaign. For the 3 weeks prior to polling day (ie during the Lib ad blitz), every day John would report to me the key findings of the polling: their attack ads were driving our vote down, our policy announcements and my performance on the road were lifting up our vote. It was a tug-o-war and they eventually won it.

As every commentator said (at the time), I outperformed Howard on the road. But obviously, their ad campaign was superior to ours. I have told you previously that, in practical terms, my involvement with the ad strategy ended on 24 August. It was Tim's job and responsibility, with the people he had assembled around him.

Having established there was no 'war-gaming' or rapid rebuttal of the Lib interest rate advertising scare campaign, Tim is now trying to make out it was my job to solve the problem with some kind of announcement during the last 9 days of the campaign. I have no recollection of a conversation with him on 29 September about an interest rate stunt or policy announcement. I saw him that afternoon but he came to show me, for information purposes, the TV ads he planned to air in the last week of the campaign. If he was so worried about interest rates, he should have showed me his rebuttal ad, but it was not part of the package. To this day, I have never seen the (delayed response) rebuttal ad that eventually went to air.

As it turned out, we didn't need negative ads in that campaign (there was no evidence in our polling that any of them worked—the Costello ones ended up being a waste of money). We did, however, need effective and rapid rebuttal ads. But we never got them in time.

My recollection is that later that week Bruce Hawker rang me with a suggestion about interest rates. He wanted us to announce a Federal equivalent of the NSW Debt Reduction Act, eventually eliminating all Commonwealth debt. Mark Arbib [Labor's NSW secretary] had been pushing the same idea with Alex Sanchez earlier in the campaign. Federal budgets, of course, are very different to the State scene and while Bruce was well intentioned, he was out of touch. He and Arbib may know about State politics but they displayed a frightening ignorance about the Federal situation.

The Liberal promise to sell Telstra would have eliminated all debt in one hit. If I had announced the Arbib/Hawker proposal, Costello and Howard would have been all over me like a rash, saying: 'Latham needs to legislate to eliminate debt but all the voters need to do is vote Coalition and endorse the full sale of Telstra. If Latham was serious, he would sell Telstra and stop pulling political stunts in the last week of an election campaign.'

Plus they would have given us a long lecture about how much (Labor) debt they had retired since 1996. Plus Treasury had been working on the debt elimination scenario, with discussion papers and seminars etc, for the previous 2 years and concluded: it may not be desirable due to the need to maintain a viable Commonwealth bond market. Shadow Treasurers McMullan and Crean had endorsed this policy position. I'm sure Hawker and Arbib had no idea this was the case.

So it was not a viable proposition. Imitating Michael Egan [the former NSW Treasurer] was not an answer, on several fronts. So I said no to Bruce, with very good reasons.

As for resigning as PM, Gartrell has a short memory. When I was Shadow Treasurer (late 2003) I asked Gartrell and Kaiser to test the following proposition: Labor is so serious about delivering surplus budgets that if it fails to do so in government, its Treasurer, Mark Latham, will resign. They came back to me and said that it was too much of a stunt and people were sceptical about it. End of story. Tim is now arguing against himself, as desperate men often do.

Even if he had put this or any other stunt to me, after the dubious value of signing the cardboard pledge earlier in the campaign, I certainly didn't want any panic-driven stunts in the last week of the campaign. We needed substance, not stunts—

hence my speech to the Press Club on 6 October outlining the comprehensive economic program I had pulled together during my time as Leader.

This is another example of the 100 'if only he had listened to me' stories since the campaign. Sure, we lost and people say that I should have done something different. In my diary I set out my own ideas on this, with the benefit of hindsight. But it doesn't mean these other people (Hawker, Arbib, Kaiser, Gartrell, McMullan, etc) are right. We won 60 seats. There was nothing to stop us from winning 50, 40 or even 30 seats if we followed flakey and poorly informed advice that was bound to backfire on us.[9]

Christmas had arrived and Latham and his party shut down. Everyone desperately hoped the holiday lull would break the circuit of Labor's infighting and that Latham would rest and return in the New Year restored, inclusive and, perhaps, contrite.

No one could know he would never return. Or that he would reject his party as unsavable.

Chapter 13

The Tsunami and the Mad End

MARK LATHAM WENT ON HOLIDAY TOWARDS THE END OF December tired, bruised by the election outcome and wanting time with Janine and his young sons. He felt he'd missed the second year of Isaac's life and was entitled to a proper holiday. He expected to be away until 26 January.

Tim Gartrell knew there were some who thought the Labor leader could not afford a long break. There was urgency, they said, to the task of rebuilding the party, wounded and weakened by the election loss. Labor's national secretary did not share their views. He felt Latham had lost some enthusiasm, was a little disengaged from the day-to-day tasks of leading and needed a decent break. Gartrell saw the year ahead as a formidable challenge to Latham's combative personality. He would need to exercise great restraint in what would be a time of finger-pointing and criticism of him. Gartrell was apprehensive. Given his prickly reaction to criticism, how would Latham cope? His leadership would be made or broken over the next twelve to eighteen months, Gartrell thought. He could have no inkling that Latham's reign would end within a month, triggered by one event far off and one in his home.

Just before 8 am on Boxing Day 2004, a catastrophic under-sea earthquake hit the northern tip of Sumatra. It measured 9.3 on the Richter scale—the equivalent of detonating 32 billion tonnes of the explosive TNT. The world's largest earthquake in forty years triggered a deadly tsunami that fanned out across the coastlines of the continents and islands that rimmed the Indian Ocean. The scale of the disaster was far from recognisable in the first days that followed. Communications had been reduced or wiped out and airfields badly damaged, hampering early on-the-ground assessments. Only slowly did the full horror emerge. Tens of thousands of Indonesians—many of them children—had been carried off by the great wave. An estimated 300 000 Indonesians, 40 000 Sri Lankans, 18 000 Indians and 10 000 Thais died. Hundreds of international tourists perished, including 21 Australians. Television footage of the tsunami's global destruction deeply moved many Australians enjoying a Christmas in prosperous times. They gave generously to appeals for help.

John Howard summoned the press to Kirribilli House the day after the tsunami hit and took charge of Australia's aid effort. The prime minister expressed Australia's sympathies to the nations that had lost so many people. His ministers mobilised and prepared to send the army, the navy and the air force into Indonesia to lead an international relief effort. Howard showed energy and spoke with compassion. The Labor leader said nothing.

What nobody outside of Latham's family knew was that between the time the tsunami hit and the dawning of its true devastation, Mark Latham had become seriously ill. The pancreatitis that felled him in August returned when he was at home, probably on 28 December—he has never confirmed the exact date. Late on that day the chairman of the Sydney Cricket Ground Trust was informed that Latham would not be making the traditional Labor leader's appearance alongside the prime minister at the New Year's Day cricket test. Though he was forced to bed with severe pain, the attack was not enough to hospitalise him and, besides, Latham knew grimly what it was. He told no one outside of his family and his doctors of the attack, although he knew it probably telegraphed the end of his political career.

He had promised Janine after the August attack that he would leave politics if there were repeat episodes. 'After my first attack of pancreatitis in August, I promised Janine that if this kept happening, I would leave politics. Realistically we didn't expect to win the election—nor did our pollster—so if the worst came to the worst and I had to leave politics, it could be handled with comparative ease from Opposition. These attacks can kill you and I would be much healthier leading a normal life outside of Parliament. No work-related risks, no Labor Party, no media bullshit. Janine, Oliver and Isaac are much bigger priorities in my life than politics and the Labor Party. So when I fell ill towards the end of 2004, it was not something I had to think a great deal about.'[1]

What he did have to think about was whether—as he and his doctors suspected—the attacks were a legacy of damage to his pancreas caused by the radiotherapy treatment he had undergone for his testicular cancer in 1992. If the answer was yes, then the attacks would be likely to continue. He underwent tests and waited for the results. He would not have them for another two weeks.

Labor's response to the rapidly worsening tsunami disaster was left to the acting party leader, Jenny Macklin, and its Foreign Affairs spokesman, Kevin Rudd. Latham's press secretary, Glenn Byres, then on holiday but monitoring the aftermath of the tsunami, knew that Labor's statements were being buried in the media and he had not detected any clamour for Latham to say something. Other senior people in the Labor Party saw it differently.

On New Year's Day, after Howard's Foreign minister Alexander Downer announced he would be going to Indonesia and Thailand to view the damage, Laurie Brereton telephoned Latham and suggested that the Labor leader issue a statement about the disaster. Latham said Macklin and Rudd had made statements on behalf of the Labor Party and that he saw no need to become involved. This was a mistake. It would soon lead to very damaging speculation and commentary about his judgement.

Latham's later emailed explanation for that decision will not appease those who believe he'd been monumentally wrong.

As for the Asian flood, Jenny Macklin was acting leader. On January 1 I advised her that I was ill. She told me that I should stay off work and she would handle things. Sounded good to me. I wasn't watching or reading that much of the media. In fact, I was blissfully out-of-touch (as is normally the case during an Australian summer). And what could I do anyway? Only the Government had the power to respond in a real way.

None of my verbiage could make any practical difference— bring back the dead, reverse the waves, organise the relief effort. Who cares what the Opposition has got to say a couple of months after an election? Only the press, talkback radio and the sticky-beaks who ring them up, the lost and lonely who have nothing else in their lives, poor bastards.

As it turned out, Macklin went on holidays herself a few days later. She obviously didn't think the Opposition had some big responsibility to discharge. In the end, I was out of there by the middle of January. A simple enough set of events. But Christ the media publish a load of rubbish, don't they. If it weren't so serious, it would be hilarious.[2]

On New Year's Day Latham also decided to tell his closest staff he was ill. Glenn Byres found the message on his mobile phone that night. Latham said he'd had another attack of pancreatitis, that it was something he would just have to deal with and that he didn't wish anything said publicly about it. From that moment, Byres believed that Latham's leadership was finished. He had known if another attack occurred Latham would most likely have to leave politics.

Latham was obsessive about keeping news of his illness restricted to his most trusted advisors for the time being. He'd sworn Jenny Macklin to secrecy. Late on New Year's Eve, the Hunter MP Joel Fitzgibbon sent Latham a New Year's text message. Latham replied to his closest friend in politics and the best man at his wedding to Janine, but made no mention of his illness. He didn't trust others in the party. 'Part of the culture of the ALP in Opposition is that people sit around all day gossiping with each other or on the phone to their journo mates. That's why I kept things tight. Imagine telling Sussex Street or the National Office or any of the machine men in caucus what was going on. I might as well have announced it on Radio 2UE.'[3]

On 2 January Latham headed off to the Star of the Sea Luxury Apartments in Terrigal for a week with Janine and the boys. They had booked the holiday months before. Latham was still unwell but they held to the plan mainly because the boys needed a break away from home. Latham emerged from their apartment to paddle in the pool with his sons—an appearance that would be later passed on to the press and used against him in the light of his silence on the tsunami.

By 3 January, speculation about Latham's whereabouts and state of mind was increasing. Alexander Downer had acted to fuel it by telling journalists as he was about to board a plane for Indonesia that the government had offered the Labor leader a briefing on the tsunami but he had not responded. Glenn Byres also became aware that Sydney's *Sun-Herald* newspaper was preparing a story likely to be critical of Latham's silence. It was obvious to Latham's staff and senior colleagues that the party would begin to suffer if the reason for his exile was not revealed.

Latham authorised Byres to brief those reporters still left in Canberra's high summer graveyard. They would be grateful for a real story. At around 6 pm on 5 January Byres put in a series of calls and told the papers of Latham's illness. He gave only the barest facts. The stories that appeared the next day were credited to a Labor source. This controlled leak was intended to buy time for Latham to continue his recovery away from the media, while he awaited the results of the medical tests that would finally decide his future.

Other senior figures in the party were advised that night that Latham was ill. Tim Gartrell listened to a cryptic message on his phone from Latham's deputy chief of staff, Simon Banks. Banks asked Gartrell to call him. 'I just want to let you know where Mark is at,' he said. Gartrell thought this meant that Latham had returned to work early and probably had some requests to make of Labor's national office. He was flabbergasted when Banks told him Latham was seriously ill.

When the news of Latham's illness finally became public Labor had a new acting leader. Chris Evans, the party's Senate leader and a little known former unionist from Western Australia, had taken over from the now holidaying Jenny Macklin. Evans used a press conference—called on the pretext of offering Labor's support to the government's tsunami relief efforts—to try and stop the fallout from Latham's silence on the tsunami by confirming his illness. Evans volunteered to the journalists present that Latham had not made a statement because his illness was painful and his doctors had told him to rest. Neither was subsequently offered as a reason by Latham. Evans had no direct contact with Latham, instead he had to rely on Latham's staff for information. The acting party leader could offer no fresh answers to the rising clamour for news about Latham's future. His frustration with questions about why there was still no tsunami statement was to show over the next few days. At a press conference on Monday 10 January, Evans curtly told a questioner: 'He's been very ill and he's off on sick leave. I think, like any other Australian, he's entitled to be on sick leave if he's sick.'

By now the crisis in federal Labor was starting to worry the Labor premiers. In Sydney, Bob Carr also called a press conference on 10 January—his first day back at work after a month in France. In keeping with past practice, Carr would have a press conference on a different subject every day during the first week of his return from holidays. He liked to remind people that he was back. But there was no escaping Latham's illness. Should Latham have made a statement on the tsunami? Was he an embarrassment to the Labor Party? Should the party change leaders? Carr batted away these unwelcome questions all week, silently frustrated that there had been no guidance from either Latham's staff nor the national office on what he should say to the press about Latham's future.

At the end of that week, Carr captured Labor's mounting agony in his dairy.

From Monday I have given the media some old fashioned razzle-dazzle. On the first day on the job I did a conference with the medical workers returning from the tsunami deluged south Asia. A few questions about how long I'd been away but the media focus on Latham—absent, said to be sick—was a snow-balling issue, rapidly overtook any issue about me. Especially as on Tuesday I had a media conference on the back-to-school allowance, Wednesday on bushfires, Thursday on prison numbers and Friday a reduction in Green slip costs that our law reforms had produced. I got back into harness. But Latham? The media turned on him viciously for being off sick, being seen on holidays with his kids, for not saying anything about the tsunami and its victims, for not being in contact with his colleagues. The result—days of Labor leadership crisis and doom for Latham who hasn't yet surfaced.

The turmoil in federal Labor was particularly sensitive in Western Australia where the Gallop Labor government was about to face a tight state election. Labor's cause there would be far from helped by the great uncertainties in the federal party. That state's attorney general, Jim McGinty, was particularly blunt, calling on Latham to consider resigning. 'The dysfunctional federal party is adding to the difficulties of state Labor governments,' he said.

Queensland's premier, Peter Beattie, had angered Latham in early December when he said he was in despair about the federal party and that he wanted Labor's federal politicians to either get rid of Latham by Christmas or declare their support for him. Now Beattie was out in public again, declaring that Beazley was the best person to assume the leadership if Latham stood aside. Carr, too, dropped his cautious position and declared that the Labor brand was suffering and the leadership had to be resolved.

The leadership crisis was fuelled by Latham late in that second week of January. He had received his test results which confirmed the fresh attack of pancreatitis was related to the damage caused by his earlier cancer treatment and therefore there was a possibility of further attacks. Latham decided he would resign the leadership and his seat, triggering a by-election. The opaque statement he released on Thursday 13 January, however, said none of this. It was deeply obscure on his health and his intentions. Joel Fitzgibbon read a draft. He thought it woefully ambiguous and that it raised more questions than it answered. He urged Latham to instead say he was looking forward to coming back to work and getting stuck into the government. Latham quietly told his friend that was not so and he couldn't lie to him. The statement read:

The news about my health has not been good. I have been told to rest and not to work—advice I am trying to follow.

Over the past fortnight I have tried to take a total break, do a few simple things with my family and to make the best recovery possible. Notwithstanding the obvious difficulties now, on the advice of my doctors and after consultation with my colleagues, I will continue this approach. I have spent this period with my family including some time at Terrigal, where I was mostly confined to our unit.

Like all Australians I reacted with horror to the unfolding tragedy of the Asian Tsunami. I feel great sympathy and grief for the victims. And I have nothing but admiration for the way the Commonwealth Government, the state governments and the Australian people have responded. Australia's response to the disaster has been magnificent.

The acting Labor leaders, Jenny Macklin and Chris Evans, have expressed these sentiments on behalf of all our members, myself included. So too, Labor expresses its grief and sympathy for the victims of the South Australian bushfires.

But in the circumstances I have been told to stay on leave and not return to work until my leave period ends on January 26. I ask the media to respect my privacy and that of my family during this period.

Aside from his offer of sympathy to the tsunami victims, eighteen days after the event, Latham's statement was a smoke-screen. He was taking himself from the leadership and the Parliament. But he had been asked by the anti-Beazley forces within the Labor Party to delay his resignation so they would have time to organise for Julia Gillard to get the leadership or deputy leadership. Latham obliged.

'The anti-Beazley forces in the caucus wanted some time to organise against him and count the numbers,' Latham said later.

Initially I was going to wait until the end of my leave period but then this wasn't necessary. They worked out they couldn't block Beazley's return. So I was free to get out which I did with a minimum amount of fuss from my point of view.

Through this period the media were such drama queens, making out that everything was in turmoil. For me, it was a period of recovery and the joy of holidaying with Janine and my two beautiful boys.

The silly media were camped outside our Glen Alpine home in 40-degree heat while I was away, taking it easy. As if I was going to talk to them when, at long last, I had some uninterrupted time with the little fellas.[4]

By now Latham was having the remotest contact with his staff and senior colleagues. He was not at home. His phone was either turned off or out of range. Gartrell never knew when Latham might call so he started leaving his mobile phone on at all hours. Latham seemed to be restricting his contact to infrequent calls to Laurie Brereton, Joel Fitzgibbon, Jenny Macklin, Gartrell and his new chief of staff, George Thompson. If one heard from Latham, he or she would ring the others. All were anxious to know his intentions. Was he really staying? Was he going? When? It was a very strange period. The Labor leader would drift in and out of contact. The Labor Party just drifted.

Three days after Latham issued his obscure statement, Joel Fitzgibbon's mobile rang at his home in the Hunter Valley, north-west of Sydney. It was a Saturday morning. Latham greeted Fitzgibbon. 'Mate, what's happening?' he asked. The question rocked Fitzgibbon, who had the doom in that morning's papers spread before him. The Labor Party and Latham were being cut to pieces on the front pages. Sydney's *Daily Telegraph* pictured Latham alongside the large headline, 'DEAD IN THE WATER'. The *Sydney Morning Herald*'s front page headline read: 'LATHAM NEEDS TO GO: STATES LEAD THE REVOLT'. *The Australian's* front page story said Beazley was ready to return to the leadership. Even Joel was quoted as saying it was responsible for ALP heavyweights to be considering leadership successors in case Latham went.

Fitzgibbon asked Latham if he'd seen the morning papers. Latham replied: 'It's out of control, isn't it. I'd better do something about it.' He told Fitzgibbon his phone battery was running low and rang off. Fitzgibbon sensed that Latham was going to do something dramatic. He suspected he might resign—not only the leadership but also his seat in Parliament. He thought to do the latter would be a mistake for Latham. Fitzgibbon called Latham back twice, leaving voice messages. There was no reply.

Fitzgibbon's hunch was right. The next day, Sunday, Tim Gartrell answered a call from Latham. 'I was one of a number of people he was calling,' Gartrell recalled. 'He'd made up his mind. He sounded in pain. His focus was on his family and there was no doubt in my mind from that conversation that the illness was extremely serious and he was being faced with a choice between a political future which would involve some health risks or a family life and a bigger guarantee about his health. He was pretty upfront. He said "I have my boys and my family to think about."

'I think he was genuinely ill and he was worried about dying, leaving the boys. He didn't say he was worried about dying, rather that was my instinct. It was like he was saying that he had a choice between family and politics and there was a risk to politics that he no longer wished to take.'[5]

The moment had come. Latham was not just resigning from the Labor leadership, after one year and one month, but also from his seat of Werriwa after eleven years in Parliament. He didn't tell Gartrell when he'd announce his resignation but Gartrell thought the next day likely. Now the machine men conferred. They accepted Latham's resignation of the leadership but they did not want a by-election in his seat so soon after the election loss and Labor's turmoil.

Gartrell spoke to Labor's NSW Branch secretary, Mark Arbib. It was agreed they'd prevail on Latham's colleagues, Laurie Brereton, Joel Fitzgibbon and John Faulkner, to try and talk Latham out of resigning from Parliament. Arbib asked Faulkner to tell Latham there was still a high probability that he'd be a minister in a future Labor government. Brereton told Arbib he believed it was all or nothing for Latham—if he couldn't be leader, he'd not stay in Parliament.

None of this worked. Latham was resolved. He later apologised to Fitzgibbon for not returning his calls. He said he didn't want to be talked out of his decision.

Monday passed and there was no word from Latham of resignation. This surprised Gartrell, who feared Latham's decision would be leaked before he could resign.

Bob Carr had been alerted on Monday night that Latham was about to resign and said so publicly the next morning.[6] Much flows from a leadership change at the top of the Labor Party. Carr was secretly planning a cabinet reshuffle that week, triggered by the impending resignation of the NSW Treasurer, Michael Egan. Carr intended to take the opportunity to shift the controversial and sometimes acerbic Michael Costa out of the state's sensitive and troublesome transport portfolio. He worried that Latham's resignation might overshadow media coverage of his ministerial reshuffle. Carr wrote in his dairy on that Monday night:

> Did a railways press conference with Costa and Vince Graham. Unbeknown to Costa, I am planning a re-shuffle. He is shifting from transport. This activated by Egan's resignation after ten years as Treasurer. I am making it a bold re-shuffle, although it might be delayed if Latham resigns as Mark Arbib says is likely. I'll put it off for a day or two.

On the morning of Tuesday 18 January Glenn Byres had just swung north onto the Hume Highway near Goulburn in the little purple Hyundai into which his tall frame squeezes when his phone rang. It was George Thompson, Latham's chief of staff. Latham would resign in the early afternoon, Thompson said, and was drafting a statement. Byres agreed to drive to the electorate office at Ingleburn in Sydney's far south-west and help arrange his boss's last press conference as Labor leader.

He was shown a draft press release. It was vintage Latham. Angry. Poignant. Direct. Thoughtful. He climbed into the media for their intrusions. He wrote simply and movingly of his love for Janine and the boys. Of his affection for the Labor Party. And of what he hoped would be his political legacy—leadership of a Labor Party that was genuinely progressive.

Latham decided to read the statement in Hallinan Park, a run-down, dried-out patch of land close to his office, bounded by a discount tyre shop and the rear of a Centrelink building. Byres and the four women who job shared in Latham's electorate office wandered down to the park for the resignation announcement. Latham had also asked his old friend, Alex Sanchez, to be there. Latham drove himself. His staff stood away from the media scramble when he arrived just before 2.30 pm wearing a blue shirt and no tie. It was his first public appearance in nearly a month. He was pale and sickly looking. His head had been almost shaved bare. His scolding of reporters and cameramen as they jostled each other for positions suggested anger. He said everything he wanted to say in less than 500 words and took no questions. He strode briskly away, looking dead ahead to his Magna, and drove himself home to the wife and two little boys he had just declared he wanted more than anything else in his life.

An epitaph for the little piece of Labor history made that afternoon in Hallinan Park might have been written long ago in the memory of Ingleburn's first doctor. Inscribed on the old, weathered sun-dial at the entrance to the park, it read:

'Grow old with me and the best is yet to come.'

Latham had walked away from the Labor Party. Kim Beazley was soon drafted back to the leadership unopposed.

The last words belong to Mark Latham.

In the circumstances, things turned out quite well. People got to see a glimpse of how Carr, Beattie and Gallop are A-grade arseholes. All their provincial bluster and posturing made no difference to anything. Never does.

The media had to sit in the heat and report a load of rubbish.

And Labor got the leader it truly deserves. The old party has become a very conservative institution, run by conservative machine men (from all factions) so it is well suited to a conservative, stand-for-nothing type of leader.

I want to make clear that I was not sorry to leave the Parliament behind. The more I saw of the inner workings of the ALP as leader, the more disillusioned I became with machine politics.

Unfortunately the ALP has become a machine political party, with each little union and each State and Territory having its own little power brokers and machine representatives in Federal caucus. I was the last of the Federal leaders not to be beholden to these roosters.

It is not an organisation that I can be optimistic about. It's beyond repair, beyond reform. That's sad for those Australians who see Labor as our best hope for social justice in this country. But I've got to be honest about it. It's a false hope. I elaborate on these matters in my diary.

Basically, the way I see it, I had my shot at being Prime Minister. It didn't work out on several fronts. But life goes on, potentially in a splendid way, spending so much time with the family. After suffering testicular cancer, the greatest gift in my life has been the ability to have children with Janine.

I would be a fool to waste it.[7]

Notes

Chapter 1 **History's Burden**
1 Bernard Lagan, 'Once Were Labor', *The Bulletin*, 19 April 2002.
2 ibid.

Chapter 4 **Sweet Summer**
1 Laurie Oakes, 'Making his Mark', *The Bulletin*, 10 December 2003.

Chapter 6 **Under the Radar**
1 Mark Latham to Bernard Lagan, 6 July 2004.
2 Dick Morris, *The New Prince: Machiavelli updated for the twenty-first century*, St Martin's Press, New York, 2000.
3 Mark Latham to Bernard Lagan, 15 June 2004.
4 Speech to National Marriage Forum, August 2004.
5 Paul Kelly, ABC–TV's *Insiders*, 8 August 2004.

Chapter 7 **A Heart in Winter**
1 Gabrielle Gwyther to Bernard Lagan. Gabrielle Gwyther remarried a western Sydney arts administrator and has a young son. She has also completed her PhD on people who live in planned estates known as gated communities.

2 Deborah Snow to Bernard Lagan, 2 September 2004.
3 Gabrielle Gwyther to Bernard Lagan, April 2004.

Chapter 8 **The Court of the King**
1 Mark Latham, email to Bernard Lagan, 6 March 2005.

Chapter 9 **The Death of the Grand Design**
1 Cherelle Murphy, *Australian Financial Review*, 25 February 2004.
2 Tim Gartrell to Bernard Lagan, 4 June 2004.
3 Mark Latham to Bernard Lagan, 13 September 2004.

Chapter 12 **The Forces are Arrayed**
1 Bob Hogg, *Australian Financial Review*, 11 October 2004.
2 Michael Costello, *The Australian*, 15 October 2004.
3 Mark Latham, email to Bernard Lagan, 19 February 2005.
4 Bob McMullan, email to Bernard Lagan, 20 April 2005.
5 Mark Latham, email to Bernard Lagan, 6 March 2005.
6 Mark Latham, email to Bernard Lagan, 19 February 2005.
7 Tim Gartrell, email to Bernard Lagan, 20 March 2005.
8 Mark Latham, email to Bernard Lagan, 19 February 2005.
9 Mark Latham, email to Bernard Lagan, 3 April 2005.

Chapter 13 **The Tsunami and the Mad End**
1 Mark Latham, email to Bernard Lagan, 19 February 2005.
2 ibid.
3 ibid.
4 ibid.
5 Tim Gartrell, interview with Bernard Lagan, 7 April 2005.
6 Bob Carr interview with Mike Carlton, Radio 2UE, 18 January
   2005.
7 Mark Latham, email to Bernard Lagan, 19 February 2005.

Acknowledgements

When I took the idea for this book to Mark Latham on a sticky day in mid-December 2003, he remarked that he might become 'King of the Fucking World' before it was released. It was, therefore, his wish that the book be published after the 2004 federal election and not before. His timing was right, his ending wrong.

We both believed then that under his leadership Labor would gain seats, if not win the election. He promised to meet me regularly to talk, off-the-record, about his progress through election year, the campaign and the aftermath. He honoured his undertaking, although after he fell seriously ill in January this year and resigned, he ended our meetings and communicated by email.

Mark Latham was the primary source for this book, which attempts to chronicle the spectacular rise and crushing fall of the man who might have been the messiah the Labor Party desperately needed. For a time it looked as though he might lead Labor into government or, at the least, slash John Howard's majority. Sadly, Latham was engulfed by electoral failure and the return of serious illness which forced him to leave politics.

This is not a one source book. I have tried wherever possible to test Mark Latham's recollections of key events with his colleagues. Inevitably, they often had different interpretations. Most people chose to co-operate only on an off-the-record basis. Again, I have endeavoured, wherever possible, to seek confirmation of their information. Invariably, the many I have approached for help with this project gave generously of their time.

I wish to thank Richard Walsh for his enthusiasm, encouragement and advice. I was also blessed with the appointment of Rebecca Kaiser of Allen & Unwin to oversee this project. I could not have asked for a finer editor.

Garry Linnell, editor of *The Bulletin*, suffered my abandonment of the magazine to take on this book with grace and encouragement. I also thank my former editors and colleagues at the *Sydney Morning Herald* for aiding my introduction to Australian political journalism.

He would not remember it but, my English teacher, Brother Roger, provided the words of encouragement that stayed with me, leading me into journalism.

Lastly, I wish to thank my lovely partner Jane Nicholls and our two daughters Grace and Rosemary, who lost me for a time when the book took over. They endured much and I shall love them always.

Bernard Lagan, May 2005

Index